101 SONNETS

Don Paterson was born in Dundee in 1963. He works as a musician and editor, and teaches at the University of St Andrews. His collection *Rain* won the Forward Prize and the Queen's Gold Medal for Poetry in 2009. His most recent book is *Reading Shakepeare's Sonnets: A New Commentary*.

by the same author

poetry
NIL NIL
GOD'S GIFT TO WOMEN
THE EYES
LANDING LIGHT
ORPHEUS
RAIN

aphorisms
THE BOOK OF SHADOWS
THE BLIND EYE

editor
101 SONNETS
ROBERT BURNS: SELECTED POEMS
LAST WORDS (with Jo Shapcott)
DON'T ASK ME WHAT I MEAN (with Clare Brown)
NEW BRITISH POETRY (with Charles Simic)

criticism
READING SHAKESPEARE'S SONNETS

101 SONNETS
from Shakespeare to Heaney

Edited with an introduction by
DON PATERSON

faber and faber

First published in 1999
by Faber and Faber Ltd
Bloomsbury House
74–77 Great Russell Street
London WC1B 3DA
This paperback edition first published in 2012

Typeset by Faber and Faber Limited
Printed and bound by CPI Group (UK) Ltd, Croydon, CRO 4YY

A CIP record for this book
is available from the British Library

ISBN 978-0-571-27873-2

Contents

Introduction

DEFINITIONS

If people can tell you one thing about a sonnet, they'll tell you it's a fourteen-line poem. But poets will tell you that a fourteen-line poem isn't necessarily a sonnet. There's a word, 'quatorzain', meaning a stanza of fourteen lines, that is also trundled out whenever someone wants to make the distinction between the sonnet 'proper' and the fourteen-line poem, though it's occasionally used just to take a poem with sonnet pretensions down a peg or two. Amongst people who have time for such things, the 'is-it-a-sonnet?' debate can rage on with all the fervour and pointlessness of country-and-western music fans trying to decide whether a record is truly 'country' or not.

The truth, these days at least, is that the sonnet is pretty much in the eye of the beholder. The form has diversified to the point where its definitive boundaries are so blurred that it has effectively ceased to exist. All we can say with any certainty is that sonnets often demonstrate certain characteristics. But these characteristics are frequently described as if they were laws: sonnets have fourteen lines. Well, actually some of them don't. They're written in iambic pentameter. Only a lot of them aren't. They rhyme according to a particular scheme. Though many of them don't, and some don't rhyme at all. They have a 'turn' – a shift in direction or tone, often further emphasized by a stanza-break – between lines 8 and 9. Though a lot of them don't. And so on. In a desperate effort to clarify things, US universities have produced statistical studies which tell us, for example, that, 'in a random sample of

7,000 sonnets, 32 per cent had the ABBAABBA CDCDCD rhyme scheme'. It might be more useful if they said, 'in a random sample of 7,000 sonnets, 6,878 were found to be terrible'. You might even go so far as to say that every really *good* sonnet seems to ignore at least one of the so-called 'rules' governing the form. A great sonnet, and I hope you'll agree that there are many in this book, will often surprise you by doing at least one thing it's not supposed to do. Though we should remember that the poet had to learn the 'rules' before they could deliberately break one of them.

So, in summary: one of the most amusing things about all the po-faced or bloody asseverations on what constitutes the 'true' sonnet is the fact that *no one* can agree on anything but the fact that it has fourteen lines. Probably. This fact still doesn't prevent certain poets and academics – even at this late hour – advancing definitions so fascistic that they would cheerfully exclude all the work of Shakespeare or Wordsworth. The only qualification for entry in this book is that the poem should have fourteen lines. Two or three poems here are probably not sonnets in anyone's book, but they are in this one: apart from being fine poems, they'll serve to show just how fuzzy the definition is.

HISTORY

Before we get on to the theoretical stuff, let's whip through the history of the form. Poets have been writing sonnets for about 750 years, and in English for around 450; in that time, the vast majority of major poets in almost every European language have written sonnets. (In Britain, only the Augustans could find no use for it – perhaps finding it ill-suited to their rather windy concerns.) It's odd, then, that some people are surprised by the fact that sonnets are still written today; if anything, the sonnet has flourished in this century, to the extent that it has become a quite unremarkable part of the contemporary poet's armoury.

The Italians were the first to recognise the potential of the sonnet. It seems certain that the sonnet has at least one of its roots in a popular Sicilian song-form, and didn't arrive entirely out of the blue. Piero delle Vigne and Giacomo da Lentini, two poets who flourished in the early thirteenth century, are often credited with its innovation – or rather with having produced the earliest sonnets as we would recognise them today. Guittone d'Arezzo (1230–94) was the first to use what we now think of as the classical Italian form of the sonnet, dividing its fourteen lines into two stanzas, rhymed ABBAABBA CDCDCD. Dante (1265–1321) and Petrarch (1304–74) brought it to an early perfection in the sonnet-cycles *Vita Nuova* and *Canzoniere* respectively, and established an early tradition for its subject matter – love. The sonnet has almost become synonymous with the love poem in the popular imagination; but things were never this straightforward, even early in the form's history. The object of Petrarch's lyric affections, Laura, puns on *laurel*; laurel wreaths were presented to poets in classical times in formal recognition of their gift (hence 'poet laureate'). Thus he conflates the idea of winning his love with that of seducing the muse through his poetic prowess. The love-sonnet has long been a way – for the male poet at least – of proving your lyric skill in the deft handling of the form, as much as winning the heart of the beloved. The exploits of the Elizabethan sonneteers, for example, have more than a whiff of testosterone-fuelled competition about them at times.

The sonnet was then steadily exported throughout the sixteenth and seventeenth centuries until it was embraced by almost the whole of Europe. Thomas Wyatt, through his virtuosic imitations of Petrarch, brought the sonnet to the English court, where Surrey innovated the so-called English form of the sonnet – three quatrains and a closing couplet, rhymed ABAB CDCD EFEF GG. Soon after, the sonnet craze broke out through the Elizabethan court like the yo-yo or the hula-hoop. It's an amazing tribute to the sonnet as a form so perfectly fitted to the shape of the human thought that it allowed poems of genius and near-genius to be written by such a tiny number of poets: the Elizabethans used it as a means of *ordering* their thought or of working out an idea, often in the form of an extended metaphor or conceit, with the argumentative inevitability of a fugue. Although the explicit subject was almost always that of love, this was often used as a pretext to write about a far wider variety of subjects – time, death, eternity and the imagination. This dissembled approach reached its apotheosis in Shakespeare's astonishing sonnet cycle, and he liberated poets thereafter to speak more directly about whatever concerned them.

In the early seventeenth century, Donne and Herbert wrote magnificent religious sonnets; Milton widened its scope, addressing political subjects and writing deeply personal sonnets of elegy and confession; his example should have allowed the sonnet to become an all-purpose occasional form. But then it fell into disuse: by the time we get to Johnson, he is able to say of the sonnet (in his *Dictionary*): 'It is not very suitable to the English language, and has not been used by any man of eminence since Milton.' (Who, as it turns out, wasn't much good either.) This is hardly likely to inspire anyone to take it up, but as

I've mentioned, the sonnet was perhaps considered too tri-
fling a form to accommodate the didactic and polemical
concerns of the era.

Few poets troubled themselves with the sonnet until it
was revived in the late eighteenth century by Bowles and
Warton (although William Lisle Bowles was highly praised
by Coleridge, neither his nor Warton's reputation has sur-
vived), and more effectively by Charlotte Smith. By the
early nineteenth century it had properly 'taken' again,
and the Romantic poets, Wordsworth and Keats in particu-
lar, brought it to new heights, expanding its repertoire by
pointing it at pretty much anything that took their fancy.
With a few notable exceptions (Hardy and Tuckerman
come to mind, though the latter was American) the
Victorians succeeded only in sentimentalising the form,
but somehow it crawled into the twentieth century intact;
thereafter the sonnet becomes so popular and varied in its
forms that its story becomes impossible and probably
pointless to delineate other than through the pages of this
book: almost every major twentieth-century poet has
written sonnets – and sonnets strictly rhymed, free-
rhymed and unrhymed, in long lines, short lines and free
verse, with stanza breaks and turns in the strangest places
imaginable.

ORIGINS

Nobody can say for certain where or when the sonnet ori-
ginated, then, but if some thirteenth-century Italian
hadn't 'invented' the sonnet, someone else would have:
we would have arrived at the sonnet as we arrived at the
wheel, out of evolutionary necessity. Not, perhaps, the
sonnet exactly as we know it – in all artistic innovation

there must be an element of the purely arbitrary – but something so close, I suspect, as to be indistinguishable from it. As poetry moved slowly off the tongue and onto the page, the visual appeal of an approximately square field of black text on a sheet of white paper must have been impossible to resist. Which is what the sonnet *is*, first and foremost: a small square poem. It presents both poet and the reader with a vivid symmetry that is the perfect emblem of the unity of meaning a sonnet seeks to embody. Unity of meaning is something that is impossible to represent in any sustained, linear, complex utterance – but it's what, crazily, our human poetry tries to do. So a sonnet is a paradox, a little squared circle, a mandala that invites our meditation.

It has the added advantage of being small enough to be easily memorised, which is the whole point of the poem – that it should lodge itself permanently in our brains. We should never forget that of all the art forms, only the poem can be carried around in the brain perfectly intact. The poem is no more or less than a little machine for remembering itself; every device and trope, whether rhyme or metre, metaphor or anaphora, or any one of the thousand others, can be said to have a mnemonic function in addition to its structural or musical one. Poetry is therefore primarily a *commemorative* act – one of committing worthwhile events and thoughts and stories to memory: its elegiac tone is so universal and pervasive we've almost stopped hearing it.

Given the length of the hendecasyllabic (eleven-syllable) line they routinely employed, it's not surprising that the early Italian poets converged on this fourteen-line form to make the square. The sonnet arrived already broken up into two quatrains and two tercets, which tells us something about its genealogy: it was most likely borrowed or adapted from an existing popular song-form. But we'll return to that fourteen in a moment.

Besides its fourteen lines, the other most common feature of the sonnet is the 'turn', or *volta*: a sudden shift in the development of the poem – a twist in the plot, or the breaking of the argument into proposition and counter-proposition, or something quieter: maybe just a shift in tone or rhetorical pitch. This is signalled explicitly in a stanza break between lines 8 and 9, implicitly by a change in the rhyme scheme, or by a clear syntactic 'signpost' at the start of line 9 – or, very often, some combination of all of the above. Sometimes the change is much more subtle, and the poem turns without indicating; it may even come slightly later or earlier than between 8 and 9 – even halfway through a line. Sometimes, though, the turn is entirely absent, especially in the kind of incantatory list-poem that works by steadily gathering momentum.

The reason we have the turn is that we just can't help it. The human brain craves disruption and variation just as much as it craves symmetry and repetition. Before we look at the various forms the sonnet can take, it's worth having a look at why the turn comes where it comes.

THE GOLDEN SECTION

Let's take a close look at the Italian sonnet, the progenitor of all the other forms. The Italian (sometimes called the 'Petrarchan', after its most famous exponent) has two stanzas: one of eight lines, generally referred to as the *octave,* followed by one of six, the *sestet.* This division is quite close to the mathematical ratio known as the golden section, or golden ratio. The mystery of the turn can't be properly understood without some discussion of this remarkable phenomenon.

The golden section is a mathematical ratio of (very) approximately 8:5, or, expressed as a decimal, 1·618 . . . It can be defined as follows: if a straight line is divided at the point where the ratio of the smaller part to the larger is the same as that of the larger to the whole, then that point occurs at the golden section. The ratio can be derived mathematically from the Fibonacci series of numbers (1, 1, 2, 3, 5, 8, 13, 21, 34, 55, etc.); each successive pair of digits slowly converges – after a bit of wobbling – more and more accurately on the ratio. Both the golden ratio and the Fibonacci series itself are omnipresent in nature: in the whorls of the pine-cone or the seedhead of the sunflower, in the number of the daisy's petals, in the spirals of the nautilus' or the snail's shell.

The golden section casts its spell over all the arts. The ratio, especially in the form of the 'golden rectangle', was often applied to the proportions of classical architecture, and was employed in the construction of the pyramids. In painting the division is often used to position the horizon line or significant detail within the picture, lending the composition an intrinsic 'rightness'. Artists from Leonardo to Seurat used the division in a highly complex way, calculating from it physical proportions, or the spatial arrangement of a picture's elements. It naturally marks the main point of dénouement in many films, dramas and operas.

Perhaps the most significant appearance of the golden section is in music. If you divide the thirteen notes of the chromatic scale from C to C at the golden section, you land on the eighth, the dominant – G. This is the first new note we encounter in the harmonic series. To oversimplify grossly: musical notes are rarely pure, and the dominant, the fifth, is the other note we tend to hear singing above the main note in a musical sound. The relationship between tonic and dominant is the basis for practically the whole of western music – and this is not dry theory, it's just the way we hear things; its rule is so pervasive that even atonal music is often rationalised by the human ear into an ebb and flow of tension and resolution between non-existent tonics and dominants. It seems reasonable to conclude that this vibrational relationship – and we're talking about *all* sounds here, not just music – must have penetrated to every part of our spiritual, mental and physical constitution.

In short, the golden section is a division we can't help making. In poetry its most explicit manifestation – there are plenty of others – is in the division of the sonnet, our square field. The reader will have already worked out that a more accurate division, according to the Fibonacci series, would have been 8:5, rather than the 8:6 we find in the sonnet. This, however, would have produced a thirteen-line poem, and superstition (for one thing, Judas was the thirteenth disciple) would have soon legislated against that form ever achieving much popularity.* Besides, as

* It might be reasonably inferred, then, that our sonnet is one line too long, and that a thirteen-line sonnet, with a turn after line 8, might be our Platonic form. Let me run this by you: one and thirteen are the same number. We often use the number twelve to indicate a cycle, so that the thirteenth instance of something brings us back to the position of the first, one rotation further on: think, for example, of the hours on the clock, the months in the year, the notes in the scale. The thirteen-line sonnet is symbolic of both transformation and unity: we've returned to precisely the same point as we started, but have ascended in pitch or moved forward in time; so in the song's singing, in the

we've seen, the sonnet was probably adapted from a handy song-form, and songs with odd number of lines in the verses are rare. (Though there *is* a thirteen-line troubadour form – the rondeau. The form is still used by poets, but its rules are too complicated to make it much more than a curiosity.)

So the division of our sonnet would have also evolved organically, even if it had begun life as a single fourteen-line stanza. As with our horizon-line, there's just a *rightness* to it: in the last century unrhymed sonnets of a single stanza often display a turn in the poem's development, quite naturally, at approximately this point. This is a feature of many longer and shorter poems too – Auden's 'Musée des Beaux Arts' is an often-cited example of a longer poem that breaks into rough sonnet proportions. All we can say with any

---

idea's thinking, something is transformed, yet stays the same. (Remember the paradox I mentioned earlier?) Or think of the musical analogy: rising to the dominant on the eighth line, pausing, and rising again to the tonic again, having ascended a full octave. (As an anecdotal aside, it's worth mentioning that many poets and musicians attest to the mysterious experience of feeling that the whole poem or composition can be inferred, with an absolute inevitability, from its very first line, or its 'given' line.)

One more thing: the spectrum, or gamut, or whole compass, can be symbolised in the number 144 – the number of completion, the big square to which all little squares (our sonnet included) perhaps aspire. Not only is 144 the square of 12, but it's the twelfth number in the Fibonacci series. Its magical potency has long been recognised: the number of saved in Revelation, for example, is 144,000; almost as many superstitions adhere to it as to the number 13.

I'd contend that what was being attempted in the sonnet-cycle (particularly in constructions like the 'corona', a series of seven sonnets, each starting with the last line of the previous one, the whole poem finishing with the very first line – though there is a more complicated scheme involving no less than fifteen sonnets), albeit unconsciously, is no less than the completion of a 144-line poem – one which ends with the same line on which the poem began, having undergone a series of profound transformations. The sonnet is a kind of minicycle, a one-octave scale as opposed to the full gamut, a symbolically curtailed 12 × 12, its own tail in its mouth on the thirteenth line (yes, okay, the fourteenth); as such it is an emblem of the mythical 144-line epic.

certainty, perhaps, is that if sonnets broke smack in the middle, they just wouldn't be any fun to write, and people wouldn't have written them.

Having said all that, we should bear in mind that our sonnet-form sits at the confluence of several forces – tradition, theory, accident, private innovation, and the more mysterious natural harmonies. To advance one cause over the others would be very misleading, but to omit one just as so.

THE FORMS OF THE SONNET

As we've mentioned, all the forms of the sonnet derive, ultimately, from the Italian sonnet. The strict form of the Italian rhymes ABBAABBA in the octave, then CDCDCD in the sestet. The English sonnet (also known as the 'Elizabethan' or 'Shakespearean') was primarily only a solution to the problem of trying to write a fourteen-line poem using only four rhymes in a language which simply doesn't have very many; to claim that it developed out of the need to find a form more fitting to the 'English' turn of mind is chauvinistic claptrap. The new rhyme-scheme goes ABAB CDCD EFEF GG. (Other solutions included a variation on the Italian, ABBA ABBA CDECDE, and Anglo-Italian schemes like ABBA ABBA CDDCEE.) As the reader can see, this naturally suggests a poem of three quatrains and a couplet; this can either be laid out in a single stanza, or broken up typographically into its constituents. The majority of English sonnets are really Italians in thin disguise; the 'turn', as we've seen, is almost a psychological inevitability in the sonnet, so although the English sonnet isn't *explicitly* broken into two stanzas, the turn frequently comes after line 8 anyway.

Often we are told that the three stanzas of the English sonnet break the argument into the neat syllogistic form of two premises and a conclusion, or the dialectical scheme of thesis, antithesis and synthesis. And, er, a bit left over. While it's true to say that the new form can certainly help the poet organise his or her thoughts in this way, the form by no means insists on it. There are far more examples of English sonnets that break this 'rule' than keep it – the 'rule' being the product of the usual mixture of wishful thinking and selective memory. (Although Shakespeare was particularly fond of setting out his stall in the first quatrain, which gives the rule some superficial credibility.) The closing couplet is a by-product of our readjusted rhyme scheme, and it can be a slightly unfortunate one if the poet takes the 'syllogism' approach too seriously. This dictates that the closing couplet should summarise the argument of the poem in a pithy and epigrammatic way, or should abstract a 'moral' from the poem. The best sonnets do nothing of the sort. Those couplets that do no more than summarise the proceedings, the Bard's included, can sound as tedious and otiose as the last line of Lear's limericks. Since poetry is largely the art of saying things once and only once, the idea of a pithy summary of the poem *within* the poem is antithetical to poetry itself, which *is* the art of pithy summary. It's interesting to look at how the most satisfying of Elizabethan English sonnets begin their final couplet with 'but' or 'and' or 'yet', where the poem is still singing the song of itself to the end – and the *least* satisfying with 'so' or 'then' or 'therefore', where the author has intruded upon the poem with two lines of redundant annotation. But when the lovely gentle click of the last couplet is allowed to close the door by itself, without the poet additionally chucking his or her weight behind it, the resulting cadence is hard to beat. We should probably remember, though, that Elizabethan readers had different expectations of their poets, and were far better able to stomach the 'moral' than we are.

In summary: these two forms – English and Italian – are still the most popular 'default' modes of the formal sonnet. The English, more often than not, turns after line 8 anyway, so it's really a hybrid; its most distinctive difference lies in the couplet, which can be a beautiful tool for effecting the closure (which can take the form of everything from the 'dying fall' of the final cadence to the 'punchline') that the very brevity of the sonnet leads us to expect.

The form of the sonnet innovated by Spenser, the 'Spenserian' sonnet, interlocks the rhymes ABABBCB-CCDCDEE, and is a good compromise between the harmonious but difficult four-rhymed Italian and the more dissipated music of the easier seven-rhymed English. The so-called 'Miltonic' sonnet is just an English sonnet without a turn, but you have to be nearly as good as Milton to pull it off. (A theory has even been advanced that fourteen unbroken lines is the human limit of sustainable lyric brilliance; the difficulty of writing a good Miltonic sonnet seems to just about prove it.) Another very popular form is the sonnet in couplets: AABBCCD-DEEFFGG. Not much has been written about it because it offers little for the idle theorist to get their teeth into; the close rhymes and absence of explicit stanza breaks make it better suited to lyric than argument, though, and it's an obvious form to choose for the list-poem, as it's easy to build up a rattling momentum.

If I were now to describe all the non-fourteen-line variations on the sonnet form, this book would go on forever. There are sonnetinos and double sonnets, cryptosonnets and curtal sonnets; the Victorian George Meredith wrote a sixteen-line sonnet for his famous sequence *Modern Love*, and in our own time, Tony Harrison has also made use of the four quatrains of the Meredithian to great effect; Hopkins wrote 'caudate' sonnets with an extra 'tail'; John Hollander has invented a thirteen-line sonnet with thirteen-syllable lines; C. K. Williams and Ciaran Carson have written long-line poems of eight and nine lines respectively that are unmistakably sonnet-like in feel. One can legitimately claim that many of these poems are as close to the spirit of the sonnet as the poems collected here; it was necessary, however, to have one inflexible law, so the rule of fourteen has been invoked.

RHYME

Academics, in particular, have talked an awful lot of rubbish on the subject of rhyme; they often make the crucial error of failing to understand that the poem ends up on the page as a result of a messy and unique process, not a single operation. This means that they often get things the wrong way round, and attribute elements that were instinctive in the composition of the poem to conscious procedures, and others that were quite deliberate to accident or instinct. The tropes and effects and schemes are described in a *post hoc*, forensic way that effectively lies to the reader about how they came into being: the rhymes of the sonnet have suffered especially from this sort of retrospective analysis. We have been told that the poet will use closely proximate rhymes to make an argument cohere, distant ones to point up contrast; but as usual, it's as easy to come up with as many examples that will disprove these theories as support them.

The truth is that most poets work to a stricter or a looser formal template, one sympathetic to the rough shape of the poem they have in their heads, then go *nose blows rose chose Montrose suppose Atholl Brose comatose* for days on end until something in them says *Bingo!* and they hit the right combination of music and sense. Poetic arguments appear to cohere simply *because* they rhyme. Rhyme *always* unifies sense, and can make sense out of nonsense; it can trick a logic from the shadows where one would not have otherwise existed. This is one of the great poetic mysteries, but here, alas, isn't the place to expand on it.

LINE

The iambic pentameter line (i.p. for short) is the commonest in use in English – that's the one that goes duh *da* duh *da* duh *da* duh *da* duh *da*. Most poetries in other languages have a line that takes up approximately the same amount of time – around three seconds or so. According to recent neurological research this would seem to have its basis in the fact that our perception of the present moment – i.e., the time we can hold in our brains as an 'instant', to be subsequently wiped or committed to the hard disk – corresponds to this length of time; this also chimes with our dictum about the poem being a machine for remembering itself.* Of course i.p. commends itself to English in many

* What we have in the sonnet, then, is approximately thirteen successive instances of the present moment. Remembering that thirteen is one, this sounds like a profoundly human spell, which is presumably why it works. The reader will have already gathered that I have the number thirteen on the brain (though in my defence, I'd contend that he or she does too), but one other thing is worth mentioning. In English poetry, if a line has an even

other ways, too: (a) it's an easy phrase length – you can train yourself to converse in it without much difficulty; and (b) iambics are the most natural meter for elegiac speech in English which, as we've seen, is practically endemic to the medium of poetry. Though triple metre (duh duh *da* duh duh *da* duh duh *da* duh duh *da*) is just as common in everyday speech, its greater speed means that it has tended to be used in lighter, humorous verse and rattling popular narratives (think of Browning's *Pied Piper*); though there's no real reason, other than convention, why its use should be restricted in this way. So – as with the sonnet – it was probably inevitable that in time we would converge on something very like this line. (Remarkably, we may even have the Italian sonneteers to thank for that too: Chaucer, who gave i.p. its big career break in the *Canterbury Tales*, may well have adapted it from his acquaintance with Petrarch and Dante following his sojourn in Italy; i.p.'s other parent was the four-stress line used in Anglo-Saxon alliterative verse.) Anyway, what we're left with is a line so amazingly flexible that our greatest writer, Shakespeare, managed to write almost his entire oeuvre using nothing else. And again, in the sonnet, the i.p. line makes for a square poem.

CONCLUSION

So by these various roads we have arrived at a miraculous little form in which our human need for unity and discon-

---

number of stresses, the natural thing to do is run on to the next without a pause between lines; if it has an *uneven* number of stresses, there's always a natural pause at the end of the line, roughly the length of another foot. The English pentameter line, then, is really twelve syllables long. The thirteenth is the start of the next line – back to one again.

tinuity, repetition and variation, tension and resolution, symmetry and asymmetry, lyric inspiration and argumentative rigour, are all held in near-perfect oppositional balance. The sonnet might be one of the greatest achievements of human ingenuity; I hope it's clear by now that it isn't some arbitrary construct that poets pit themselves against out of a perverse sense of craftsmanlike duty – it's a box for their dreams, and represents one of the most characteristic shapes human thought can take. Poets write sonnets because it makes poems easier to write. Readers read them because it makes their lives easier to bear.

101 SONNETS

The Silken Tent

She is as in a field a silken tent
At midday when a sunny summer breeze
Has dried the dew and all its ropes relent,
So that in guys it gently sways at ease,
And its supporting central cedar pole,
That is its pinnacle to heavenward
And signifies the sureness of the soul,
Seems to owe naught to any single cord,
But strictly held by none, is loosely bound
By countless silken ties of love and thought
To everything on earth the compass round,
And only by one's going slightly taut
In the capriciousness of summer air
Is of the slightest bondage made aware.

In Her Praise

This they know well: the Goddess yet abides.
Though each new lovely woman whom she rides,
Straddling her neck a year or two or three,
Should sink beneath such weight of majesty
And, groping back to humankind, gainsay
The headlong power that whitened all her way
With a broad track of trefoil – leaving you,
Her chosen lover, ever again thrust through
With daggers, your purse rifled, your rings gone –
Nevertheless they call you to live on
To parley with the pure, oracular dead,
To hear the wild pack whimpering overhead,
To watch the moon tugging at her cold tides.
Woman is mortal woman. She abides.

Muse

When I kiss you in all the folding places
of your body, you make that noise like a dog
dreaming, dreaming of the long runs he makes
in answer to some jolt to his hormones,
running across landfills, running, running
by tips and shorelines from the scent of too much,
but still going with head up and snout
in the air because he loves it all
and has to get away. I have to kiss deeper
and more slowly – your neck, your inner arm,
the neat creases under your toes, the shadow
behind your knee, the white angles of your groin –
until you fall quiet because only then
can I get the damned words to come into my mouth.

To His Maistres

So swete a kis yistrene fra thee I reft,
In bowing down thy body on the bed,
That evin my lyfe within thy lippis I left;
Sensyne from thee my spirits wald never shed;
To folow thee it from my body fled,
And left my corps als cold as ony kie.
Bot when the danger of my death I dred,
To seik my spreit I sent my harte to thee;
Bot it wes so inamored with thyn ee,
With thee it myndit likwyse to remane:
So thou hes keepit captive all the thrie,
More glaid to byde then to returne agane.
Except thy breath thare places had suppleit,
Even in thyn armes, thair doutles had I deit.

yistrene: last night; *kie*: key

Maundy Thursday

Between the brown hands of a server-lad
The silver cross was offered to be kissed.
The men came up, lugubrious, but not sad,
And knelt reluctantly, half-prejudiced.
(And kissing, kissed the emblem of a creed.)
Then mourning women knelt; meek mouths they had,
(And kissed the Body of the Christ indeed.)
Young children came, with eager lips and glad.
(These kissed a silver doll, immensely bright.)
Then I, too, knelt before that acolyte.
Above the crucifix I bent my head:
The Christ was thin, and cold, and very dead:
And yet I bowed, yea, kissed – my lips did cling
(I kissed the warm live hand that held the thing.)

'Batter my heart, three-personed God'

Batter my heart, three-personed God; for, you
As yet but knock, breathe, shine, and seek to mend;
That I may rise, and stand, o'erthrow me, and bend
Your force, to break, blow, burn and make me new.
I, like an usurpt town, to another due,
Labour to admit you, but Oh, to no end.
Reason, your viceroy in me, me should defend,
But is captiv'd, and proves weak or untrue.
Yet dearly I love you, and would be loved fain,
But am betrothed unto your enemy:
Divorce me, untie or break that knot again,
Take me to you, imprison me, for I
Except you enthrall me, never shall be free,
Nor ever chaste, except you ravish me.

Upon the Crucifix

Now I have found thee, I will evermore
Embrace this standard where thou sitst above.
Feed greedy eyes and from hence never rove,
Suck hungry soul of this eternal store,
Issue my heart from thy two-leaved door,
And let my lips from kissing not remove.
O that I were transformèd into love,
And as a plant might spring upon this flower;
Like wandering ivy or sweet honeysuckle,
How would I with my twine about it buckle,
And kiss his feet with my ambitious boughs,
And climb along upon his sacred breast,
And make a garland for his wounded brows.
Lord, so I am if here my thoughts might rest.

Arsehole

It is shy as a gathered eyelet
neatly worked in shrinking violet;
it is the dilating iris, tucked
away, a tightening throb when fucked.

It is a soiled and puckered hem,
the golden treasury's privy purse.
With all the colours of a bruise,
it is the fleck of blood in albumen.

I dreamed your body was an instrument
and this was the worn mouthpiece
to which my breathing lips were bent.

Each note pleaded to love a little longer,
longer, as though it was dying of hunger.
I fed that famished mouth my ambergris.

Delight in Disorder

A sweet disorder in the dress
Kindles in clothes a wantonness:
A lawn about the shoulders thrown
Into a fine distraction:
An erring lace which here and there
Enthralls the crimson stomacher:
A cuff neglectful, and thereby
Ribbons to flow confusedly:
A winning wave, deserving note,
In the tempestuous petticoat:
A careless shoe-string, in whose tie
I see a wild civility:
Do more bewitch me than when art
Is too precise in every part.

An Enigma

'Seldom we find,' says Solomon Don Dunce,
'Half an idea in the profoundest sonnet.
Through all the flimsy things we see at once
As easily as through a Naples bonnet –
Trash of all trash? – how *can* a lady don it?
Yet heavier far than your Petrarchan stuff –
Owl-downy nonsense that the faintest puff
Twirls into trunk-paper while you con it.'
And, veritable, Sol is right enough.
The general tuckermanities are arrant
Bubbles – ephemeral and *so* transparent –
But *this* is, now, – you may depend on it –
Stable, opaque, immortal – all by dint
Of the dear names that lie concealed within't.

'The world is too much with us'

The world is too much with us; late and soon,
Getting and spending, we lay waste our powers:
Little we see in Nature that is ours;
We have given our hearts away, a sordid boon!
This Sea that bares her bosom to the moon;
The winds that will be howling at all hours,
And are up-gathered now like sleeping flowers;
For this, for everything, we are out of tune;
It moves us not. – Great God! I'd rather be
A Pagan suckled in a creed outworn;
So might I, standing on this pleasant lea,
Have glimpses that would make me less forlorn;
Have sight of Proteus rising from the sea;
Or hear old Triton blow his wreathèd horn.

'Two voices are there: one is of the deep'

Two voices are there: one is of the deep;
It learns the storm-cloud's thunderous melody,
Now roars, now murmurs with the changing sea,
Now bird-like pipes, now closes soft in sleep:
And one is of an old half-witted sheep
Which bleats articulate monotony,
And indicates that two and one are three,
That grass is green, lakes damp, and mountains steep:

And, Wordsworth, both are thine: at certain times
Forth from the heart of thy melodious rhymes
The form and pressure of high thoughts will burst:
At other times – good Lord! I'd rather be
Quite unacquainted with the A. B. C.
Than write such hopeless rubbish as thy worst.

'Not the round natural world, not the deep mind'

Not the round natural world, not the deep mind,
The reconcilement holds: the blue abyss
Collects it not; our arrows sink amiss
And but in Him may we our import find.
The agony to know, the grief, the bliss
Of toil, is vain and vain: clots of the sod
Gathered in heat and haste and flung behind
To blind ourselves and others, what but this
Still grasping dust and sowing toward the wind?
No more thy meaning seek, thine anguish plead,
But leaving straining thought and stammering word,
Across the barren azure pass to God;
Shooting the void in silence like a bird,
A bird that shuts his wings for better speed.

The Poem that Took the Place of a Mountain

There it was, word for word,
The poem that took the place of a mountain.

He breathed its oxygen,
Even when the book lay turned in the dust of his table.

It reminded him how he had needed
A place to go to in his own direction,

How he had recomposed the pines,
Shifted the rocks and picked his way among clouds,

For the outlook that would be right,
Where he would be complete in an unexplained completion:

The exact rock where his inexactnesses
Would discover, at last, the view toward which they had
    edged,

Where he could lie and, gazing down at the sea,
Recognize his unique and solitary home.

The Book of the World

Of this fair volume which we World do name
If we the sheets and leaves could turn with care,
Of him who it corrects and did it frame,
We clear might read the art and wisdom rare:
Find out his power which wildest powers doth tame,
His providence existing everywhere,
His justice which proud rebels doth not spare,
In every page, no, period of the same.
But silly we, like foolish children, rest
Well pleased with coloured vellum, leaves of gold,
Fair dangling ribands, leaving what is best,
On the great writer's sense ne'er taking hold;
Or if by chance our minds do muse on ought,
It is some picture on the margin wrought.

SEAN O'BRIEN

from Notes on the Use of the Library
(Basement Annexe)

For John Bagnall

The Principal's other edition of Q,
Scott by the truckload, and Fredegond Shove,
Manuals instructing the dead how to do
What they no longer can with the Torments of Love,
Mistaken assumptions concerning The Race,
Twelve-volume memoirs of footling campaigns,
Discredited physics, the Criminal Face,
Confessions of clerics who blew out their brains,
Laws and Geographies (utterly changed),
Travellers' journals that led up the creek,
The verbose, the inept and the clearly deranged,
The languages no one has bothered to speak,
And journals of subjects that do not exist:
What better excuse to go out and get pissed?

Régime de Vivre

I rise at eleven, I dine about two,
I get drunk before seven, and the next thing I do,
I send for my whore, when for fear of a clap,
I spend in her hand, and I spew in her lap;
Then we quarrel and scold, till I fall fast asleep,
When the bitch growing bold, to my pocket does creep.
Then slyly she leaves me, and to revenge the affront,
At once she bereaves me of money and cunt.
If by chance then I wake, hot-headed and drunk,
What a coil do I make for the loss of my punk!
I storm, and I roar, and I fall in a rage.
And missing my whore, I bugger my page.
Then crop-sick all morning I rail at my men,
And in bed I lie yawning till eleven again.

Still-Life

Through the open french window the warm sun
lights up the polished breakfast-table, laid
round a bowl of crimson roses, for one –
a service of Worcester porcelain, arrayed
near it a melon, peaches, figs, small hot
rolls in a napkin, fairy rack of toast,
butter in ice, high silver coffee pot,
and, heaped on a salver, the morning's post.

She comes over the lawn, the young heiress,
from her early walk in her garden-wood
feeling that life's a table set to bless
her delicate desires with all that's good,

that even the unopened future lies
like a love-letter, full of sweet surprise.

'If there were, oh! an Hellespont of cream'

The author loving these homely meats specially, viz.:
cream, pancakes, buttered pippin-pies (laugh, good people)
and tobacco; writ to that worthy and virtuous gentle-
woman, whom he calleth mistress, as followeth

If there were, oh! an Hellespont of cream
Between us, milk-white mistress, I would swim
To you, to show to both my love's extreme,
Leander-like, – yea! dive from brim to brim.
But met I with a buttered pippin-pie
Floating upon 't, that would I make my boat
To waft me to you without jeopardy,
Though sea-sick I might be while it did float.
Yet if a storm should rise, by night or day,
Of sugar-snows and hail of caraways,
Then, if I found a pancake in my way,
It like a plank should bring me to your kays;
    Which having found, if they tobacco kept,
    The smoke should dry me well before I slept.

Guava Libre

for Jane Fonda, Leningrad, 1975

Pickled Gold Coast clitoridectomies?
Labia minora in formaldehyde?
A rose pink death mask of a screen cult kiss,
Marilyn's mouth or vulva mummified?

Lips cropped off a poet. That's more like.
That's almost the sort of poet I think I am.
The lips of Orpheus fished up by a dyke
singing 'Women of Cuba Libre and Vietnam!'

The taste, though, taste! Ah, that could only be

('Women! Women! O *abajo* men,
the thought of it's enough to make you come!')

the honeyed yoni of Eurydice

and I am Orpheus going down again –

Thanks for the guavas soaked in Cuban rum.

To a Goose

If thou didst feed on western plains of yore
Or waddle wide with flat and flabby feet
Over some Cambrian mountain's plashy moor,
Or find in farmer's yard a safe retreat
From gipsy thieves and foxes sly and fleet;
If thy grey quills by lawyer guided, trace
Deeds big with ruin to some wretched race,
Or love-sick poet's sonnet, sad and sweet,
Wailing the rigour of some lady fair;
Or if, the drudge of housemaid's daily toil,
Cobwebs and dust thy pinion white besoil,
Departed goose! I neither know nor care.
But this I know, that thou wert very fine
Seasoned with sage and onions and port wine.

Fly

A fat fly fuddles for an exit
at the window-pane.
Bluntly, stubbornly, it inspects it,
like a brain
nonplussed by a seemingly simple sentence
in a book,
which the glaze of unduly protracted acquaintance
has turned to gobbledygook.

A few inches above where the fly fizzes
a gap of air
waits, but this has
not yet been vouchsafed to the fly.
Only retreat and a loop or swoop of despair
will give it the sky.

Honey Cycle

Grisaille of gristle lights, in a high cyc of cells,
ex-chrysalids being fed-crystal in six-sided wells,
many sweating comb and combing it, seating it sexaplex.
The unique She sops lines of descent, in her comedown from
    sex
and drones are driven from honey, having given their own:
their oeuvre with her ova or not, he's re-learn the lone.
Rules never from bees but from being give us to build food
then to be stiff guards, hairtrigger for tiffs with non-Brood.
Next, grid-eyes grown to gathering rise where a headwind
    bolsters
hung shimmering flight, return with rich itchy holsters
and dance the nectar vector. Bristling collectors they
    entrance
propel off, our stings strung. And when we its advance
beyond wings, or water, light gutters in our sight-lattice
and we're eggs there again. Spent fighting-suits tighten in
    grass.

The Soote Season

The soote season, that bud and bloom forth brings,
With green hath clad the hill and eke the vale,
The nightingale with feathers new she sings;
The turtle to her make hath told her tale.
Summer is come, for every spray now springs;
The hart hath hung his old head on the pale;
The buck in brake his winter coat he flings;
The fishes flete with new-repairèd scale;
The adder all her slough away she slings;
The swift swallow pursueth the flies smale;
The busy bee her honey now she mings;
Winter is worn that was the flowers' bale.
    And thus I see among these pleasant things
    Each care decays, and yet my sorrow springs.

soote: sweet; *make*: mate; *flete*: float; *smale*: small; *mings*: mixes

SAMUEL TAYLOR COLERIDGE

Work without Hope
Lines composed 21st February 1825

All Nature seems at work. Slugs leave their lair –
The bees are stirring – birds are on the wing –
And Winter slumbering in the open air,
Wears on his smiling face a dream of Spring!
And I, the while, the sole unbusy thing,
Nor honey make, nor pair, nor build, nor sing.

Yet well I ken the banks where amaranths blow,
Have traced the fount whence streams of nectar flow.
Bloom, O ye amaranths! bloom for whom ye may,
For me ye bloom not! Glide, rich streams, away!
With lips unbrightened, wreathless brow, I stroll:
And would you learn the spells that drowse my soul?
Work without Hope draws nectar in a sieve,
And Hope without an object cannot live.

The Melancholy Year

The melancholy year is dead with rain.
Drop after drop on every branch pursues.
From far away beyond the drizzled flues
A twilight saddens to the window pane.
And dimly thro' the chambers of the brain,
From place to place and gently touching, moves
My one and irrecoverable love's
Dear and lost shape one other time again.
So in the last of autumn for a day
Summer or summer's memory returns.
So in a mountain desolation burns
Some rich belated flower, and with the gray
Sick weather, in the world of rotting ferns
From out the dreadful stones it dies away.

Grief

I tell you, hopeless grief is passionless;
That only men incredulous of despair,
Half-taught in anguish, through the midnight air
Beat upward to God's throne in loud access
Of shrieking and reproach. Full desertness
In souls, as countries, lieth silent-bare
Under the blanching, vertical eye-glare
Of the absolute Heavens. Deep-hearted man, express
Grief for thy Dead in silence like to death:
Most like a monumental statue set
In everlasting watch and moveless woe,
Till itself crumble to the dust beneath.
Touch it: the marble eyelids are not wet;
If it could weep, it could arise and go.

'Striving to sing glad songs, I but attain'

Striving to sing glad songs, I but attain
Wild discords sadder than Grief's saddest tune;
As if an owl with his harsh screech should strain
To over-gratulate a thrush of June.
The nightingale upon its thorny spray
Finds inspiration in the sullen dark;
The kindling dawn, the world-wide joyous day
Are inspiration to the soaring lark;
The seas are silent in the sunny calm,
Their anthem surges in the tempest boom;
The skies outroll no solemn thunder psalm
Till they have clothed themselves with clouds of gloom.
My mirth can laugh and talk, but cannot sing;
My grief finds harmonies in everything.

Cheap Seats, the Cincinnati Gardens, Professional Basketball, 1959

The less we paid, the more we climbed. Tendrils
of smoke lazed just as high and hung there, blue,
particulate, the opposite of dew.
We saw the whole court from up there. Few girls
had come, few wives, numerous boys in molt
like me. Our heroes leapt and surged and looped
and two nights out of three, like us, they'd lose.
But 'like us' is wrong: we had no result
three nights out of three: so we had heroes.
And 'we' is wrong, for I knew none by name
among the hazy company unless
I brought her with me. This was loneliness
with noise, unlike the kind I had at home
with no clock running down, and mirrors.

Opera

Throw all your stagey chandeliers in wheelbarrows and
    move them north
To celebrate my mother's sewing-machine
And her beneath an eighty-watt bulb, pedalling
Iambs on an antique metal footplate
Powering the needle through its regular lines,
Doing her work. To me as a young boy
That was her typewriter. I'd watch
Her hands and feet in unison, or read
Between her calves the wrought-iron letters:
SINGER. Mass-produced polished wood and metal,
It was a powerful instrument. I stared
Hard at its brilliant needle's eye that purred
And shone at night; and then each morning after
I went to work at school, wearing her songs.

Those Winter Sundays

Sundays too my father got up early
and put his clothes on in the blueblack cold,
then with cracked hands that ached
from labor in the weekday weather made
banked fires blaze. No one ever thanked him.

I'd wake and hear the cold splintering, breaking.
When the rooms were warm, he'd call,
and slowly I would rise and dress,
fearing the chronic angers of that house,

Speaking indifferently to him,
who had driven out the cold
and polished my good shoes as well.
What did I know, what did I know
of love's austere and lonely offices?

To His Sonne

Three thinges there bee that prosper up apace
And flourish, whilest they growe a sunder farr,
But on a day, they meet all in one place,
And when they meet, they one an other marr;
And they bee theise, the wood, the weede, the wagg.
The wood is that, which makes the Gallow tree,
The weed is that, which stringes the Hangmans bagg,
The wagg my pritty knave betokeneth thee.
Marke well deare boy whilest theise assemble not,
Green springs the tree, hempe growes, the wagg is wilde,
But when they meet, it makes the timber rott,
It frets the halter, and it choakes the childe.
 Then bless thee, and beware, and lett us praye,
 Wee part not with thee at this meeting day.

'Long time a child'

Long time a child, and still a child, when years
Had painted manhood on my cheek, was I, –
For yet I lived like one not born to die;
A thriftless prodigal of smiles and tears,
No hope I needed, and I knew no fears.
But sleep, though sweet, is only sleep; and waking,
I waked to sleep no more; at once o'ertaking
The vanguard of my age, with all arrears
Of duty on my back. Nor child, nor man,
Nor youth, nor sage, I find my head is gray,
For I have lost the race I never ran:
A rathe December blights my lagging May;
And still I am a child, though I be old:
Time is my debtor for my years untold.

For My Daughter

Looking into my daughter's eyes I read
Beneath the innocence of morning flesh
Concealed, hintings of death she does not heed.
Coldest of winds have blown this hair, and mesh
Of seaweed snarled these miniatures of hands;
The night's slow poison, tolerant and bland,
Has moved her blood. Parched years that I have seen
That may be hers appear: foul, lingering
Death in certain war, the slim legs green.
Or, fed on hate, she relishes the sting
Of others' agony; perhaps the cruel
Bride of a syphilitic or a fool.
These speculations sour in the sun.
I have no daughter. I desire none.

The Brother

Dropping a canapé in my beaujolais
At some reception, opening or launch,
I recall briefly the brother I never had
Presiding at less worldly rituals:
The only man at my wedding not wearing a tie;
Avuncular, swaddling my nephew over the font;
Thumbing cool oil on our mother's forehead
In the darkened room, the bells and frankincense . . .
While the prodigal sweats in the strip-lit corridor.

Now, picture us facing each other, myself and the brother
I never met: two profiles in silhouette,
Or else a chalice, depending how you look.
Imagine that's this polystyrene cup.
I must break bread with my own flesh and blood.

The Bright Field

I have seen the sun break through
to illuminate a small field
for a while, and gone my way
and forgotten it. But that was the pearl
of great price, the one field that had
the treasure in it. I realize now
that I must give all that I have
to possess it. Life is not hurrying

on to a receding future, nor hankering after
an imagined past. It is the turning
aside like Moses to the miracle
of the lit bush, to a brightness
that seemed as transitory as your youth
once, but is the eternity that awaits you.

JOHN CLARE

Noon

The mid day hour of twelve the clock counts oer
A sultry stillness lulls the air asleep
The very buzz of flye is heard no more
Nor one faint wrinkle oer the waters creep
Like one large sheet of glass the pool does shine
Reflecting in its face the burnt sun beam
The very fish their sturting play decline
Seeking the willow shadows side the stream
And where the awthorn branches oer the pool
The little bird forsaking song and nest
Flutters on dripping twigs his limbs to cool
And splashes in the stream his burning breast
O free from thunder for a sudden shower
To cherish nature in this noon day hour

The Halted Moment

Wha hasna turn'd inby a sunny street
And fund alang its length nae folk were there:
And heard his step fa' steadily and clear
Nor wauken ocht but schedows at his feet.
Shüther to shüther in the reemlin heat
The houses seem'd to hearken and to stare;
But a' were doverin whaur they stüde and were
Like wa's ayont the echo o' time's beat.
Wha hasna thocht whan atween stanes sae still,
That had been biggit up for busyness,
He has come wanderin into a place
Lost, and forgotten, and unchangeable:
And thocht the far-off traffic sounds to be
The weary waters o' mortality.

wauken: woken; *ocht*: anything; *shüther*: shoulder;
reemlin: tremulous; *dovering*: dozing; *biggit*: built

'A Sonnet is a moment's monument'

A Sonnet is a moment's monument, –
Memorial from the Soul's eternity
To one dead deathless hour. Look that it be,
Whether for lustral rite or dire portent,
Or its own arduous fullness reverent:
Carve it in ivory or in ebony
As Day or Night shall rule; and let Time see
Its flowering crest impearled and orient.
A sonnet is a coin: its face reveals
The soul, – its converse, to what Power 'tis due:
Whether for tribute to the august appeals
Of Life, or dower in Love's high retinue
It serve, or, mid the dark wharf's cavernous breath,
In Charon's palm it pay the toll to Death.

Ad Lectorem de Subiecto Operis Sui

The little world the subject of my muse,
Is an huge task and labour infinite;
Like to a wilderness or mass confuse,
Or to an endless gulf, or to the night:
How many strange meanders do I find?
How many paths do turn my straying pen?
How many doubtful twilights make me blind,
Which seek to limn out this strange All of men?
Easy it were the earth to portray out,
Or to draw forth the heavens' purest frame,
Whose restless course by order whirls about
Of change and place, and still remains the same.
But how shall men's, or manners' form appear,
Which while I write, do change from what they were?

Opening the Cage

14 variations on 14 words

I have nothing to say and I am saying it and that is poetry.
John Cage

I have to say poetry and is that nothing and am I saying it
I am and I have poetry to say and is that nothing saying it
I am nothing and I have poetry to say and that is saying it
I that am saying poetry have nothing and it is I and to say
And I say that I am to have poetry and saying it is nothing
I am poetry and nothing and saying it is to say that I have
To have nothing is poetry and I am saying that and I say it
Poetry is saying I have nothing and I am to say that and it
Saying nothing I am poetry and I have to say that and it is
It is and I am and I have poetry saying say that to nothing
It is saying poetry to nothing and I say I have and am that
Poetry is saying I have it and I am nothing and to say that
And that nothing is poetry I am saying and I have to say it
Saying poetry is nothing and to that I say I am and have it

Inniskeen Road: July Evening

The bicycles go by in twos and threes –
There's a dance in Billy Brennan's barn tonight,
And there's the half-talk code of mysteries
And the wink-and-elbow language of delight.
Half-past eight and there is not a spot
Upon a mile of road, no shadow thrown
That might turn out a man or woman, not
A footfall tapping secrecies of stone.

I have what every poet hates in spite
Of all the solemn talk of contemplation.
Oh, Alexander Selkirk knew the plight
Of being king and government and nation.
A road, a mile of kingdom, I am king
Of banks and stones and every blooming thing.

The Laurel Axe

Autumn resumes the land, ruffles the woods
with smoky wings, entangles them. Trees shine
out from their leaves, rocks mildew to moss-green;
the avenues are spread with brittle floods.

Platonic England, house of solitudes,
rests in its laurels and its injured stone,
replete with complex fortunes that are gone,
beset by dynasties of moods and clouds.

It stands, as though at ease with its own world,
the mannerly extortions, languid praise,
all that devotion long since bought and sold,

the rooms of cedar and soft-thudding baize,
tremulous boudoirs where the crystals kissed
in cabinets of amethyst and frost.

In the Lost Province

As it comes back, brick by smoky brick,
I say to myself – strange I lived there
And walked those streets. It is the Ormeau Road
On a summer's evening, a haze of absence
Over the caked city, that slumped smell
From the blackened gasworks. Ah, those brick canyons
Where Brookeborough unsheathes a sabre,
Shouting 'No Surrender' from the back of a lorry.

And the sky is a dry purple, and men
Are talking politics in a back room.
Is it too early or too late for change?
Certainly the province is most peaceful.
Who would dream of necessity, the angers
Of Leviathan, or the years of judgement?

CHARLOTTE SMITH

Written in the Church Yard at Middleton in Sussex

Pressed by the moon, mute arbitress of tides,
    While the loud equinox its power combines,
    The sea no more its swelling surge confines,
But o'er the shrinking land sublimely rides.
The wild blast, rising from the western cave,
    Drives the huge billows from their heaving bed,
    Tears from their grassy tombs the village dead,
And breaks the silent sabbath of the grave!
With shells and sea-weed mingled, on the shore
    Lo! their bones whiten in the frequent wave;
    But vain to them the winds and waters rave;
They hear the warring elements no more:
While I am doomed – by life's long storm oppressed,
To gaze with envy on their gloomy rest.

February Afternoon

Men heard this roar of parleying starlings, saw,
A thousand years ago even as now,
Black rooks with white gulls following the plough
So that the first are last until a caw
Commands that last are first again, – a law
Which was of old when one, like me, dreamed how
A thousand years might dust lie on his brow
Yet thus would birds do between hedge and shaw.

Time swims before me, making as a day
A thousand years, while the broad ploughland oak
Roars mill-like and men strike and bear the stroke
Of war as ever, audacious or resigned,
And God still sits aloft in the array
That we have wrought him, stone-deaf and stone-blind.

PERCY BYSSHE SHELLEY

Ozymandias

I met a traveller from an antique land
Who said: Two vast and trunkless legs of stone
Stand in the desert. Near them, on the sand,
Half sunk, a shattered visage lies, whose frown,
And wrinkled lip, and sneer of cold command,
Tell that its sculptor well those passions read
Which yet survive, stamped on these lifeless things,
The hand that mocked them and the heart that fed;
And on the pedestal these words appear:
'My name is Ozymandias, king of kings:
Look on my works, ye Mighty, and despair!'
Nothing beside remains. Round the decay
Of that colossal wreck, boundless and bare
The lone and level sands stretch far away.

Mythology

Penelope as a *garçon manqué*
weaves sonnets on a barstool among sailors.
tapping her iambs out on the brass rail. Ours
is not the high-school text. Persephone
a.k.a. Télémaque-who-tagged-along,
sleeps off her lunch on an Italian train
headed for Paris, while Ulysse-Maman
plugs into the Shirelles singing her song
('What Does a Girl Do?'). What *does* a girl do
but walk across the world, her kid in tow,
stopping at stations on the way, with friends
to tie her to the mast when she gets too
close to the edge? And when the voyage ends,
what does a girl do? Girl, that's up to you.

Leda and the Swan

A sudden blow: the great wings beating still
Above the staggering girl, her thighs caressed
By the dark webs, her nape caught in his bill,
He holds her helpless breast upon his breast.

How can those terrified vague fingers push
The feathered glory from her loosening thighs?
And how can body, laid in that white rush,
But feel the strange heart beating where it lies?

A shudder in the loins engenders there
The broken wall, the burning roof and tower
And Agamemnon dead.
                              Being so caught up,
So mastered by the brute blood of the air,
Did she put on his knowledge with his power
Before the indifferent beak could let her drop?

She, to Him (iii)

I will be faithful to thee; aye, I will!
And Death shall choose me with a wondering eye
That he did not discern and domicile
One his by right ever since that last Good-bye!

I have no care for friends, or kin, or prime
Of manhood who deal gently with me here;
Amid the happy people of my time
Who work their love's fulfilment, I appear

Numb as a vane that cankers on its point,
True to the wind that kissed ere canker came:
Despised by souls of Now, who would disjoint
The mind from memory, making Life all aim,

My old dexterities in witchery gone,
And nothing left for Love to look upon.

'Since there's no help, come let us kiss and part'

Since there's no help, come let us kiss and part, –
Nay I have done, you get no more of me;
And I am glad, yea glad with all my heart,
That thus so cleanly I myself can free;
Shake hands for ever, cancel all our vows,
And when we meet at any time again,
Be it not seen in either of our brows
That we one jot of former love retain.
Now at the last gasp of Love's latest breath,
When, his pulse failing, Passion speechless lies,
When Faith is kneeling by his bed of death,
And Innocence is closing up his eyes, –
Now if thou would'st, when all have given him over,
From death to life thou might'st him yet recover!

'You must not wonder though you think it strange'

You must not wonder though you think it strange
To see me hold my lowring head so low,
And that mine eyes take no delight to range
About the gleams which on your face do grow.
The mouse which once hath broken out of trap
Is seldom teased with the trustless bait,
But lies aloof for fear of more mishap
And feedeth still in doubt of deep deceit.
The scorched fly which once hath 'scaped the flame
Will hardly come to play again with fire.
Whereby I learn that grievous is the game
Which follows fancy dazzled by desire.
   So that I wink or else hold down my head
   Because your blazing eyes my bale have bred.

'Their faces shone under some radiance'

Their faces shone under some radiance
Of mingled moonlight and lamplight
That turned the empty kisses into meaning,
The island of such penny love
Into a costly country, the graves
That neighboured them to wells of warmth,
(And skeletons had sap). One minute
Their faces shone; the midnight rain
Hung pointed in the wind,
Before the moon shifted and the sap ran out,
She, in her cheap frock, saying some cheap thing,
And he replying,
Not knowing radiance came and passed.
The suicides parade again, now ripe for dying.

Death

It is not death, that sometime in a sigh
   This eloquent breath shall take its speechless flight;
That sometime these bright stars, that now reply
   In sunlight to the sun, shall set in night;
   That this warm conscious flesh shall perish quite,
And all life's ruddy springs forget to flow;
   That thoughts shall cease, and the immortal sprite
Be lapp'd in alien clay and laid below;
It is not death to know this – but to know
   That pious thoughts, which visit at new graves
In tender pilgrimage, will cease to go
   So duly and so oft – and when grass waves
Over the pass'd-away, there may be then
No resurrection in the minds of men.

After Death

The curtains were half drawn, the floor was swept
    And strewn with rushes, rosemary and may
    Lay thick upon the bed on which I lay,
Where through the lattice ivy-shadows crept.
He leaned above me, thinking that I slept
    And could not hear him; but I heard him say:
    'Poor child, poor child:' and as he turned away
Came a deep silence, and I knew he wept.
He did not touch the shroud, or raise the fold
    That hid my face, or take my hand in his,
      Or ruffle the smooth pillows for my head:
      He did not love me living; but once dead
    He pitied me; and very sweet it is
To know he still is warm though I am cold.

JAMIE MCKENDRICK

Ye Who Enter In
(after Antonio Machado)

To plumb the depths of hell and meet
ministers, saladins and scholars,
Marilyn Monroe and Cleopatra,
the latter naked as the day they died;
to give audience where you please
and where you don't to curl your lip
or deftly rabbit-punch a kidney
sure that your arm is power-assisted.
To be steered about by someone who just
happens to be Virgil, and you like his poems.
To write as a chisel writes on rock
so every phrase you write resounds forever:
ABANDON ALL HOPE . . . You first.
No really I insist please after you.

Karma

Christmas was in the air and all was well
With him, but for a few confusing flaws
In divers of God's images. Because
A friend of his would neither buy nor sell,
Was he to answer for the axe that fell?
He pondered; and the reason for it was,
Partly, a slowly freezing Santa Claus
Upon the corner, with his beard and bell.

Acknowledging an improvident surprise,
He magnified a fancy that he wished
The friend whom he had wrecked were here again.
Not sure of that, he found a compromise;
And from the fulness of his heart he fished
A dime for Jesus who had died for men.

Finding the Ox

A Zen warrior searches for inner peace.
His bow is like a harp, that he might twang its string
In lonely combat with himself, and so release
The arrow of desire. An archer should want nothing.

His is the blue music of what is happening.
His sword rings true. Its many lives of hammered steel
Were there before him, and he trusts its weighty swing.
He knows the rallentando of a roulette wheel,

Or red leaves floating in a stream of eau de nil,
Bisected by a showy rival blade, while his
The leaves avoided. He's the opposite of zeal.

When he aims at the bull he closes his eyes.
Sometimes he hits it dead-on with a mighty whizz.
Sometimes he's way off target, which is no surprise.

Swineherd

'When all this is over,' said the swineherd,
'I mean to retire, where
Nobody will have heard about my special skills
And conversation is mainly about the weather.

I intend to learn how to make coffee, at least as well
As the Portuguese lay-sister in the kitchen
And polish the brass fenders every day.
I want to lie awake at night
Listening to cream crawling to the top of the jug
And the water lying soft in the cistern.

I want to see an orchard where the trees grow in straight
    lines
And the yellow fox finds shelter between the navy-blue
    trunks,
Where it gets dark early in summer
And the apple-blossom is allowed to wither on the bough.'

'I dreamt he drove me back to the asylum'

I dreamt he drove me back to the asylum
Straight after lunch; we stood then at one end,
A sort of cafeteria behind, my friend
Behind me, nuts in groups about the room;
A dumbwaiter with five shelves was waiting (some-
thing's missing here) to take me up – I bend
And lift a quart of milk to hide and tend,
Take with me. Everybody is watching, dumb.

I try to put it first among some worm-
shot volumes of the N.E.D. I had
On the top shelf – then somewhere else . . . slowly
Lise comes up in a matron's uniform
And with a look (I saw once) infinitely sad
In her grey eyes takes it away from me.

My Turn

I have been so enchanted by the girls
who have a hunch, I have been seen

following them to the red and green
see-saws. There have been a few of them

I recognised. I have been recognised.
I have stood on the roundabout and turned.

I have swung, uselessly, not as high as them.
Then seen the parents coming, and the rain

on rusty and unmanned remaining things.
I have calculated west from the light cloud.

Cried myself dry and jumped
back on the roundabout when it had stopped.

Started it again, in the dark wet,
with my foot down, then both my feet on it.

Farewell to Juliet

I see you, Juliet, still, with your straw hat
Loaded with vines, and with your dear pale face,
On which those thirty years so lightly sat,
And the white outline of your muslin dress.
You wore a little *fichu* trimmed with lace
And crossed in front, as was the fashion then,
Bound at your waist with a broad band or sash,
All white and fresh and virginally plain.
There was a sound of shouting far away
Down in the valley, as they called to us,
And you, with hands clasped seeming still to pray
Patience of fate, stood listening to me thus
With heaving bosom. There a rose lay curled.
It was the reddest rose in all the world.

'When I have fears that I may cease to be'

When I have fears that I may cease to be
   Before my pen has glean'd my teeming brain,
Before high-piled books, in charactery,
   Hold like rich garners the full ripen'd grain;
When I behold, upon the night's starr'd face,
   Huge cloudy symbols of a high romance,
And think that I may never live to trace
   Their shadows, with the magic hand of chance;
And when I feel, fair creature of an hour,
   That I shall never look upon thee more,
Never have relish in the faery power
   Of unreflecting love; – then on the shore
Of the wide world I stand alone, and think
Till love and fame to nothingness do sink.

'I read my sentence – steadily'

I read my sentence – steadily –
Reviewed it with my eyes,
To see that I made no mistake
In its extremest clause –
The Date, and manner, of the shame –
And then the Pious Form
That 'God have mercy' on the Soul
The Jury voted Him –
I made my soul familiar – with her extremity –
That at the last, it should not be a novel Agony –
But she, and Death, acquainted –
Meet tranquilly, as friends –
Salute, and pass, without a Hint –
And there, the Matter ends –

JOSEPH BLANCO WHITE

To Night

Mysterious Night! when our first parent knew
    Thee from report divine, and heard thy name,
    Did he not tremble for this lovely frame,
This glorious canopy of light and blue.
Yet 'neath a curtain of translucent dew,
    Bathed in the rays of the great setting flame,
    Hesperus with the host of heaven came,
And lo! creation widened in man's view.
Who could have thought such darkness lay concealed
    Within thy beams, O Sun! or who could find,
Whilst fly and leaf and insect stood revealed,
    That to such countless orbs thou mad'st us blind!
        Why do we then shun Death with anxious strife?
        If Light can thus deceive, wherefore not Life?

'Care-charmer Sleep, son of the sable Night'

Care-charmer Sleep, son of the sable Night,
Brother to Death, in silent darkness born,
Relieve my languish, and restore the light;
With dark forgetting of my care return,
And let the day be time enough to mourn
The shipwreck of my ill-adventured youth:
Let waking eyes suffice to wail their scorn,
Without the torment of the night's untruth.
Cease, dreams, the images of day-desires,
To model forth the passions of the morrow;
Never let rising Sun approve you liars,
To add more grief to aggravate my sorrow:
   Still let me sleep, embracing clouds in vain,
   And never wake to feel the day's disdain.

Now Sleeps the Crimson Petal

Now sleeps the crimson petal, now the white;
Nor waves the cypress in the palace walk;
Nor winks the gold fin in the porphyry font:
The fire-fly wakens: waken thou with me.

Now droops the milkwhite peacock like a ghost,
And like a ghost she glimmers on to me.

Now lies the Earth all Danaë to the stars,
And all thy heart lies open unto me.

Now slides the silent meteor on, and leaves
A shining furrow, as thy thoughts in me.

Now folds the lily all her sweetness up,
And slips into the bosom of the lake:
So fold thyself, my dearest, thou, and slip
Into my bosom and be lost in me.

PAUL MULDOON

The Princess and the Pea

This is no dream
By Dulac out of the Brothers Grimm,
A child's disquiet,
Her impish mouth,
The quilt upon embroidered quilt
Of satin and shot silk,
Her lying there, extravagant, aloof,
Like cream on milk.

This is the dream of her older sister,
Who is stretched on the open grave
Of all the men she has known.
Far down, something niggles. The stir
Of someone still alive.
Then a cry, far down. It is your own.

'I, being born a woman and distressed'

I, being born a woman and distressed
By all the needs and notions of my kind,
Am urged by your propinquity to find
Your person fair, and feel a certain zest
To bear your body's weight upon my breast:
So subtly is the fume of life designed,
To clarify the pulse and cloud the mind,
And leave me once again undone, possessed.
Think not for this, however, the poor treason
Of my stout blood against my staggering brain,
I shall remember you with love, or season
My scorn with pity, – let me make it plain:
I find this frenzy insufficient reason
For conversation when we meet again.

ANTHONY HECHT

An Old Malediction
(*freely from Horace*)

What well-heeled knuckle-head, straight from the unisex
Hairstylist and bathed in *Russian Leather*,
Dallies with you these late summer days, Pyrrha,
In your expensive sublet? For whom do you
Slip into something simple by, say, Gucci?
The more fool he who has mapped out for himself
The saline latitudes of incontinent grief.
Dazzled though he be, poor dope, by the golden looks
Your locks fetched up out of a bottle of *Clairol*,
He will know that the wind changes, the smooth sailing
Is done for, when the breakers wallop him broadside,
When he's rudderless, dismasted, thoroughly swamped
In that mindless rip-tide that got the best of me
Once, when I ventured on your deeps, Piranha.

Elegy

They are lang deid, folk that I used to ken,
their firm-set lips aa mowdert and agley,
sherp-tempert een rusty amang the cley:
they are baith deid, thae wycelike, bienlie men,

heidmaisters, that had been in pouer for ten
or twenty year afore fate's taiglie wey
brocht me, a young, weill-harnit, blate and fey
new-cleckit dominie, intill their den.

Ane tellt me it was time I learnt to write –
round-haund, he meant – and saw about my hair:
I mind of him, beld-heidit, wi a kyte.

Ane sneerit quarterly – I cuidna square
my savings bank – and sniftert in his spite.
Weill, gin they arena deid, it's time they were.

mowdert: mouldering; *agley*: awry; *wycelike*: sensible;
bienlie: healthy, prosperous; *taiglie*: tangled;
weill-harnit: well-schooled; *blate*: shy;
new-cleckit: newly hatched; *kyte*: paunch; *gin*: if

GEORGE MACKAY BROWN

The Death of Peter Esson
Tailor, Town Librarian, Free Kirk Elder

Peter at some immortal cloth, it seemed,
Fashioned and stitched, for so long had he sat
Heraldic on his bench. We never dreamed
It was his shroud that he was busy at.

Well Peter knew, his thousand books would pass
Gray into dust, that still a tinker's tale
As hard as granite and as sweet as grass,
Told over reeking pipes, outlasts them all.

The Free Kirk cleaves grey houses – Peter's ark
Freighted for heaven, galeblown with psalm and prayer.
The predestined needle quivered on the mark.
The wheel spun true. The seventieth rock was near.

Peter, I mourned. Early on Monday last
There came a wave and stood above your mast.

The Fall

The bloudy trunck of him who did possesse
    Above the rest a haplesse happy state,
This little Stone doth Seale, but not depresse,
    And scarce can stop the rowling of his fate.

Brasse Tombes which justice hath deny'd t'his fault,
    The common pity to his vertues payes,
Adorning an Imaginary vault,
    Which from our minds time strives in vaine to raze.

Ten yeares the world upon him falsly smil'd,
    Sheathing in fawning lookes the deadly knife
Long aymed at his head; That so beguild
    It more securely might bereave his Life.

Then threw him to a Scaffold from a Throne.
Much Doctrine lyes under this little Stone.

CATHERINE DYER

Epitaph on the Monument of Sir William Dyer at Colmworth, 1641

My dearest dust, could not thy hasty day
Afford thy drowszy patience leave to stay
One hower longer: so that we might either
Sate up, or gone to bedd together?
But since thy finisht labor hath possest
Thy weary limbs with early rest,
Enjoy it sweetly: and thy widdowe bride
Shall soone repose her by thy slumbring side.
Whose business, now, is only to prepare
My nightly dress, and call to prayre:
Mine eyes wax heavy and ye day growes cold.
Draw, draw ye closed curtaynes: and make room:
My deare, my dearest dust; I come, I come.

On His Deceased Wife

Methought I saw my late espousèd saint
    Brought to me like Alcestis from the grave,
    Whom Jove's great son to her glad husband gave,
    Rescued from death by force, though pale and faint.
Mine, as whom washed from spot of child-bed taint
    Purification in the old law did save;
    And such, as yet once more I trust to have
    Full sight of her in heaven without restraint,
Came vested all in white, pure as her mind:
    Her face was veiled, yet to my fancied sight
    Love, sweetness, goodness, in her person shined
So clear, as in no face with more delight.
    But oh! as to embrace me she inclined,
    I waked, she fled, and day brought back my night.

The Rites for Cousin Vit

Carried her unprotesting out the door.
Kicked back the casket-stand. But it can't hold her,
That stuff and satin aiming to enfold her,
The lid's contrition nor the bolts before.
Oh oh. Too much. Too much. Even now, surmise,
She rises in the sunshine. There she goes,
Back to the bars she knew and the repose
In love-rooms and the things in people's eyes.
Too vital and too squeaking. Must emerge.
Even now she does the snake-hips with a hiss,
Slops the bad wine across her shantung, talks
Of pregnancy, guitars and bridgework, walks
In parks or alleys, comes haply on the verge
Of happiness, haply hysterics. Is.

Poem

And if it snowed and snow covered the drive
he took a spade and tossed it to one side.
And always tucked his daughter up at night.
And slippered her the one time that she lied.

And every week he tipped up half his wage.
And what he didn't spend each week he saved.
And praised his wife for every meal she made.
And once, for laughing, punched her in the face.

And for his mum he hired a private nurse.
And every Sunday taxied her to church.
And he blubbed when she went from bad to worse.
And twice he lifted ten quid from her purse.

Here's how they rated him when they looked back:
sometimes he did this, sometimes he did that.

Who's Who

A shilling life will give you all the facts:
How Father beat him, how he ran away,
What were the struggles of his youth, what acts
Made him the greatest figure of his day:
Of how he fought, fished, hunted, worked all night,
Though giddy, climbed new mountains; named a sea:
Some of the last researchers even write
Love made him weep his pints like you and me.

With all his honours on, he sighed for one
Who, say astonished critics, lived at home;
Did little jobs about the house with skill
And nothing else; could whistle; would sit still
Or potter round the garden; answered some
Of his long marvellous letters but kept none.

Grace Darling

After you had steered your coble out of the storm
And left the smaller islands to break the surface,
Like draughts shaking that colossal backcloth there came
Fifty pounds from the Queen, proposals of marriage.

The daughter of a lighthouse-keeper and the saints
Who once lived there on birds' eggs, rainwater, barley
And built to keep all pilgrims at a safe distance
Circular houses with views only of the sky,

Who set timber burning on the top of a tower
Before each was launched at last in his stone coffin –
You would turn your back on mainland and suitor
To marry, then bereave the waves from Lindisfarne,

A moth against the lamp that shines still and reveals
Many small boats at sea, lifeboats, named after girls.

'One day I wrote her name upon the strand'

One day I wrote her name upon the strand,
    But came the waves and washed it away:
Again I wrote it with a second hand,
    But came the tide and made my pains his prey.
    Vain man (said she), that dost in vain assay
A mortal thing so to immortalise;
    For I myself shall like to this decay,
And eke my name be wiped out likewise.
Not so (quod I); let baser things devise
    To die in dust, but you shall live by fame;
My verse your virtues rare shall eternise,
    And in the heavens write your glorious name:
      Where, whenas death shall all the world subdue,
      Our love shall live, and later life renew.

from Strugnell's Sonnets

Not only marble, but the plastic toys
From cornflake packets will outlive this rhyme:
I can't immortalize you, love – our joys
Will lie unnoticed in the vault of time.
When Mrs Thatcher has been cast in bronze
And her administration is a page
In some O-level text-book, when the dons
Have analysed the story of our age,
When travel firms sell tours of outer space
And aeroplanes take off without a sound
And Tulse Hill has become a trendy place
And Upper Norwood's on the underground
Your beauty and my name will be forgotten –
My love is true, but all my verse is rotten.

'That time of year thou mayst in me behold'

That time of year thou mayst in me behold,
When yellow leaves, or none, or few do hang
Upon those boughs which shake against the cold,
Bare ruined choirs where late the sweet birds sang;
In me thou seest the twilight of such day
As after sunset fadeth in the west,
Which by and by black night doth take away
Death's second self that seals up all in rest;
In me thou seest the glowing of such fire
That on the ashes of his youth doth lie,
As the deathbed, whereon it must expire,
Consumed with that which it was nourished by;
This thou perceiv'st, which makes thy love more
      strong,
To love that well, which thou must leave ere long.

A Virginal

No, no! Go from me. I have left her lately.
I will not spoil my sheath with lesser brightness,
For my surrounding air hath a new lightness;
Slight are her arms, yet they have bound me straitly
And left me cloaked as with a gauze of æther;
As with sweet leaves; as with subtle clearness.
Oh, I have picked up magic in her nearness
To sheathe me half in half the things that sheathe her.
No, no! Go from me. I have still the flavour,
Soft as spring wind that's come from birchen bowers.
Green come the shoots, aye April in the branches,
As winter's wound with her sleight hand she staunches,
Hath of the trees a likeness of the savour:
As white their bark, so white this lady's hours.

'Whoso list to hunt, I know where is an hind'

Whoso list to hunt, I know where is an hind,
But as for me, helas, I may no more.
The vain travail hath wearied me so sore,
I am of them that farthest cometh behind.
Yet may I by no means my wearied mind
Draw from the deer, but as she fleeth afore
Fainting I follow. I leave off therefore
Sithens in a net I seek to hold the wind.
Who list her hunt, I put him out of doubt,
As well as I may spend his time in vain.
And graven with diamonds in letters plain
There is written her fair neck round about:
'*Noli me tangere* for Caesar's I am,
And wild for to hold though I seem tame.'

'To Speak of the Woe That is In Marriage'

*It is the future generation that presses into being by means
of these exuberant feelings and supersensible soap bubbles
of ours.*   Schopenhauer

'The hot night makes us keep our bedroom windows open.
Our magnolia blossoms. Life begins to happen.
My hopped up husband drops his home disputes,
and hits the streets to cruise for prostitutes,
free-lancing out along the razor's edge.
This screwball might kill his wife, then take the pledge.
Oh the monotonous meanness of his lust . . .
It's the injustice . . . he is so unjust –
whiskey-blind, swaggering home at five.
My only thought is how to keep alive.
What makes him tick? Each night now I tie
ten dollars and his car key to my thigh . . .
Gored by the climacteric of his want,
he stalls above me like an elephant.'

Modern Love

It is summer, and we are in a house
That is not ours, sitting at a table
Enjoying minutes of a rented silence,
The upstairs people gone. The pigeons lull
To sleep the under-tens and invalids,
The tree shakes out its shadows to the grass,
The roses rove through the wilds of my neglect.
Our lives flap, and we have no hope of better
Happiness than this, not much to show for love
Than how we are, or how this evening is,
Unpeopled, silent, and where we are alive
In a domestic love, seemingly alone,
All other lives worn down to trees and sunlight,
Looking forward to a visit from the cat.

Lucifer in Starlight

On a starred night Prince Lucifer uprose.
Tired of his dark dominion swung the fiend
Above the rolling ball in cloud part screened,
Where sinners hugged their spectre of repose.
Poor prey to his hot fit of pride were those.
And now upon his western wing he leaned,
Now his huge bulk o'er Afric's sands careened,
Now the black planet shadowed Arctic snows.
Soaring through wider zones that pricked his scars
With memory of the old revolt from Awe,
He reached a middle height, and at the stars,
Which are the brain of heaven, he looked, and sank.
Around the ancient track marched, rank on rank,
The army of unalterable law.

'Satan, no woman, yet a wandering spirit'

Satan, no woman, yet a wandering spirit,
When he saw ships sail two ways with one wind,
Of sailors' trade he hell did disinherit:
The Devil himself loves not a half-fast mind.

The satyr when he saw the shepherd blow
To warm his hands, and make his pottage cool,
Manhood forswears, and half a beast did know,
Nature with double breath is put to school.

Cupid doth head his shafts in women's faces,
Where smiles and tears dwell ever near together,
Where all the arts of change give passion graces;
While these clouds threaten, who fears not the weather?
    Sailors and satyrs, Cupid's knights, and I,
        Fear women that swear, Nay; and know they lie.

MARK ALEXANDER BOYD

Sonet

Fra banc to banc, fra wod to wod, I rin
Ourhailit with my feble fantasie,
Lyc til a leif that fallis from a trie
Or til a reid ourblawin with the wind.
Twa gods gyds me: the ane of tham is blind,
Yea, and a bairn brocht up in vanitie;
The next a wyf ingenrit of the se,
And lichter nor a dauphin with hir fin.

Unhappie is the man for evirmaire
That teils the sand and sawis in the aire;
Bot twyse unhappier is he, I lairn,
That feidis in his hairt a mad desyre,
And follows on a woman throw the fyre,
Led be a blind and teachit be a bairn.

> *ourhailit*: overcome; *til*: to; *wyf*: woman;
> *ingenrit*: engendered; *teils*: tells

'With how sad steps, O moon, thou climb'st the skies'

With how sad steps, O Moon, thou climb'st the skies!
   How silently, and with how wan a face!
   What! may it be that even in heavenly place
That busy archer his sharp arrows tries?
Sure, if that long-with-love-acquainted eyes
   Can judge of love, thou feel'st a lover's case.
   I read it in thy looks. Thy languisht grace
To me that feel the like, thy state descries.
   Then even of fellowship, O Moon, tell me
Is constant love deemed there but want of wit?
   Are beauties there as proud as here they be?
Do they above love to be loved, and yet
   Those lovers scorn whom that love doth possess?
   Do they call virtue there, ungratefulness?

Friday Night in the Royal Station Hotel

Light spreads darkly downwards from the high
Clusters of lights over empty chairs
That face each other, coloured differently.
Through open doors, the dining-room declares
A larger loneliness of knives and glass
And silence laid like carpet. A porter reads
An unsold evening paper. Hours pass,
And all the salesmen have gone back to Leeds,
Leaving full ashtrays in the Conference Room.

In shoeless corridors, the lights burn. How
Isolated, like a fort, it is –
The headed paper, made for writing home
(If home existed) letters of exile: *Now
Night comes on. Waves fold behind villages.*

Sunday Morning

Down the road someone is practising scales,
The notes like little fishes vanish with a wink of tails,
Man's heart expands to tinker with his car
For this is Sunday morning, Fate's great bazaar;
Regard these means as ends, concentrate on this Now,
And you may grow to music or drive beyond Hindhead
    anyhow,
Take corners on two wheels until you go so fast
That you can clutch a fringe or two of the windy past,
That you can abstract this day and make it to the week of
    time
A small eternity, a sonnet self-contained in rhyme.

But listen, up the road, something gulps, the church spire
Opens its eight bells out, skulls' mouths which will not tire
To tell how there is no music or movement which secures
Escape from the weekday time. Which deadens and endures.

Prayer

Some days, although we cannot pray, a prayer
utters itself. So, a woman will lift
her head from the sieve of her hands and stare
at the minims sung by a tree, a sudden gift.

Some nights, although we are faithless, the truth
enters our hearts, that small familiar pain;
then a man will stand stock-still, hearing his youth
in the distant Latin chanting of a train.

Pray for us now. Grade I piano scales
console the lodger looking out across
a Midlands town. Then dusk, and someone calls
a child's name as though they named their loss.

Darkness outside. Inside, the radio's prayer –
Rockall. Malin. Dogger. Finisterre.

Prayer

Prayer the Churches banquet, Angels age,
   God's breath in man returning to his birth,
   The soul in paraphrase, heart in pilgrimage,
The Christian plummet sounding heav'n and earth;
Engine against th'Almightie, sinners towre,
   Reversèd thunder, Christ-side-piercing spear,
   The six-daies world transposing in an houre,
A kinde of tune, which all things heare and fear;
Softnesse, and peace, and joy, and love, and blisse,
   Exalted Manna, gladnesse of the best,
   Heaven in ordinarie, man well drest,
The milkie way, the bird of Paradise,
   Church-bels beyond the starres heard, the souls bloud,
   The land of spices; something understood.

BARNABE BARNES

'A blast of wind, a momentary breath'

A blast of wind, a momentary breath,
A watery bubble symbolised with air,
A sun-blown rose, but for a season fair,
A ghostly glance, a skeleton of death;
A morning dew, pearling the grass beneath,
Whose moisture sun's appearance doth impair;
A lightning glimpse, a muse of thought and care,
A planet's shot, a shade which followeth,
A voice which vanishes so soon as heard
The thriftless heir of time, a rolling wave,
A show, no more in action than regard,
A mass of dust, world's momentary slave,
 Is man, in state of our old Adam made,
 Soon born to die, soon flourishing to fade.

Praise in Summer

Obscurely yet most surely called to praise,
As sometimes summer calls us all, I said
The hills are heavens full of branching ways
Where star-nosed moles fly overhead the dead;
I said the trees are mines in air, I said
See how the sparrow burrows in the sky!
And then I wondered why this mad *instead*
Perverts our praise to uncreation, why
Such savor's in this wrenching things awry.
Does sense so stale that it must needs derange
The world to know it? To a praiseful eye
Should it not be enough of fresh and strange
That trees grow green, and moles can course in clay,
And sparrows sweep the ceiling of our day?

ELIZABETH BISHOP

Sonnet

Caught – the bubble
in the spirit-level,
a creature divided;
and the compass needle
wobbling and wavering,
undecided.
Freed – the broken
thermometer's mercury
running away;
and the rainbow-bird
from the narrow bevel
of the empty mirror,
flying wherever
it feels like, gay!

GERARD MANLEY HOPKINS

'As kingfishers catch fire, dragonflies dráw fláme'

As kingfishers catch fire, dragonflies dráw fláme;
As tumbled over rim in roundy wells
Stones ring; like each tucked string tells, each hung bell's
Bow swung finds tongue to fling out broad its name;
Each mortal thing does one thing and the same:
Deals out that being indoors each one dwells;
Selves – goes itself; *myself* it speaks and spells,
Crying *Whát I do is me: for that I came.*

Í say móre: the just man justices;
Kéeps gráce: thát keeps all his goings graces;
Acts in God's eye what in God's eye he is –
Chríst – for Christ plays in ten thousand places,
Lovely in limbs, and lovely in eyes not his
To the Father through the features of men's faces.

To the Evening Star

Thou fair-hair'd angel of the evening,
Now, whilst the sun rests on the mountains, light
Thy bright torch of love; thy radiant crown
Put on, and smile upon our evening bed!
Smile on our loves, and while thou drawest the
Blue curtains of the sky, scatter thy silver dew
On every flower that shuts its sweet eyes
In timely sleep. Let thy west wind sleep on
The lake; speak silence with thy glimmering eyes,
And wash the dusk with silver. Soon, full soon,
Dost thou withdraw; then the wolf rages wide,
And the lion glares thro' the dun forest:
The fleeces of our flocks are cover'd with
Thy sacred dew: protect them with thine influence.

Rag and Bone

That sun ray has raced to us
at those millions of miles an hour.
But when it reaches the floor of the room
it creeps slower than a philosopher,
it makes a bright puddle
that alters like an amoeba,
it climbs the door
as though it were afraid it would fall.

In a few minutes it'll make this page
an assaulting dazzle. I'll pull a curtain
sideways. I'll snip
a few yards off those millions of miles
and, tailor of the universe, sit quietly
stitching my few ragged days together.

The Skylight

You were the one for skylights. I opposed
Cutting into the seasoned tongue-and-groove
Of pitch pine. I liked it low and closed,
Its claustrophobic, nest-up-in-the-roof
Effect. I liked the snuff-dry feeling,
The perfect, trunk-lid fit of the old ceiling.
Under there, it was all hutch and hatch.
The blue slates kept the heat like midnight thatch.

But when the slates came off, extravagant
Sky entered and held surprise wide open.
For days I felt like an inhabitant
Of that house where the man sick of the palsy
Was lowered through the roof, had his sins forgiven,
Was healed, took up his bed and walked away.

3 ROBERT FROST: *The Silken Tent* For my money, one of the most
brilliantly sustained conceits in the English language, and as fine a
love poem as you'll ever read. An English sonnet, as quietly virtuosic
as they come – look at the way, for example, Frost enacts the tautening
of one of the 'silken ties' in line 12 by throwing an extra stress on 'one's'
in 'by one's going', when we expect an unstressed syllable.

4 ROBERT GRAVES: *In Her Praise* Graves very much in White Goddess
overdrive; though real women get typically short shrift in the poem, it
nonetheless must chime with a lot of real men's experience of falling in
love. A sonnet in couplets with the turn between lines 9 and 10.

5 JO SHAPCOTT: *Muse* A successful poet–muse relationship usually
depends on the muse shutting up altogether: male poets have found all
sorts of ways to guarantee this – falling in love with someone who
won't speak to them, someone who's very far away, non-existent, or
dead. Here the situation seems gender-reversed as the woman in the
poem tries to silence her lover, so *she* can speak; but it's more
complicated than this. Who *is* the muse here? An unrhymed one
stanza-sonnet, with the turn halfway through line 9.

6 ALEXANDER MONTGOMERIE: *To His Maistres* Montgomerie
was just about the last of the *makars*, poets who wrote in Lowland Scots
in the sixteenth century. He wrote a number of fine sonnets, usually
favouring the Spenserian stanza with its ABABBCBCCDCDEE rhyme
scheme. The poet leaves his mistress with, in turn, his life, his spirit
and his heart: he was probably quite relieved that the sonnet wasn't
four lines longer. The couplet ties up the conceit beautifully.

7 WILFRED OWEN: *Maundy Thursday* This poem is usually filed
under Owen's juvenilia, but juvenilia seems a bit of a luxury when you
die at twenty-five. What we are meant to read into the last line is
ambiguous; the poem coincides with Owen's disenchantment with
Christianity. An Italian sonnet with no turn, and the sestet arranged
in couplets.

8 JOHN DONNE: '*Batter my heart, three-personed God*' The intensity, at
least, of Donne's sexual metaphor seems to be largely subconscious.

Remarkable in that, as usual, Donne seems to be running two or three metaphors concurrently without mixing any of them. Note especially how the poem immediately declares its passion with the inversion of the first iamb, so that it starts with a strong rather than a weak stress, and then crams six strong stresses into the second line.

9 WILLIAM ALABASTER: *Upon the Crucifix* Phew! This makes Donne's 'Batter my heart...' look like page three of the *Church Times*. One of a series of sonnets on the symbols of the passion, but could reasonably be read as a gay love poem re-addressed to Christ for the sake of discretion. An Italian sonnet, but much too feverish to have time for the turn.

10 CRAIG RAINE: *Arsehole* Yes, well. This is a very loose imitation of a poem by the French symbolist poet Arthur Rimbaud, beginning '*Obscur et fronce comme un oeillet violet...*' After the clever descriptions of the octave, the poem manages to convey a genuinely tender lyric yearning, quite an accomplishment under the circumstances.

11 ROBERT HERRICK: *Delight in Disorder* The Cavalier poet and occasional clergyman is unusual amongst poets in that his work is generally quite, well, cheerful. This sonnet is unorthodox in its use of a tetrameter (four-stress) line instead of the usual pentameter, giving it the light song-like quality possessed by many of Herrick's lyrics, which have often been set to music.

12 EDGAR ALLAN POE: *An Enigma* Just a bit of fun, this one: buried in the poem is the name of the woman to whom the poem is addressed – a simple key unlocks it. And I'm not giving it to you.

13 WILLIAM WORDSWORTH: '*The world is too much with us*' A terrific Italian sonnet, with the turn coming half a line later than usual and all the more effective for it. Note especially the way Wordsworth communicates his frustration by wrestling with the meter in lines 2 and 3, reversing the initial iamb so that each line starts with a strong stress. Proteus was Poseidon's sealherd, 'the old man of the sea', and Triton another minor sea-deity, who could calm the waters by sounding a blast on his conch-shell.

14 J. K. STEPHEN: '*Two voices are there: one is of the deep*' An Italian sonnet with an enjoyably nasty surprise in the turn.

15 FREDERICK GODDARD TUCKERMAN: '*Not the round natural world, not the deep mind*' From *Sonnets*, First Series. Although he's been lately

rescued from complete obscurity, the American Tuckerman is still one of the most seriously undervalued poets of the nineteenth century. A great innovator in the sonnet form, Tuckerman's work is unusual in that his meditations seem to be addressed to no one but himself, and are largely free of the hysterical apostrophising that characterised many of the sonnets of the time. This is a free-rhymed sonnet, with the turn between lines 9 and 10, and a muscularly syncopated use of stress against the pentameter rhythm, reminiscent of Hopkins.

16 WALLACE STEVENS: *The Poem That Took the Place of a Mountain* This is probably a sonnet only by wilful designation. But it's as clear and unified a statement as Stevens ever made on one of his obsessive themes: how the word and the world lie superimposed on one another, and what happens when the mind gets between them.

17 WILLIAM DRUMMOND OF HAWTHORNDEN: *The Book of the World* Hawthornden was the first Scot deliberately to set about writing poems in English. This is an Italian sonnet with a closing couplet; the poem tricks out the conceit in masterly style – with a good twist at the turn, and then another little twist again on the couplet.

18 SEAN O'BRIEN: *Note on the Use of the Library (Basement Annexe)* An unusual English sonnet – a list-poem written in triple-meter. This rhythm (often inaccurately called anapaestic – we should stop) is often associated with lighter subjects and popular verse forms; although this poem is essentially a laugh, it has a black edge to it – and in other poems by O'Brien he has turned the meter to much darker and more serious ends.

19 JOHN WILMOT, EARL OF ROCHESTER: *Régime de Vivre* Rochester was a court poet of considerable talent, and quite possibly the rudest in history. He embarked on his career of epic debauchery at the age of twelve, and was dead of syphilis by thirty-two. His deathbed renunciation of atheism is either famous or notorious, depending on your capacity for cynicism. This jaunty effort is unusual for a sonnet in that it's written in triple-metre – anapaests in old money.

20 ELIZABETH DARYUSH: *Still-Life* The best breakfast ever described, though by the end of the poem you want to go at it with a cricket bat. It's hard to know *exactly* where the poet stands on all this, but we can perhaps sense her disapproval in the pampered insularity of the scene. I hope. A nice Anglo-Italian sonnet, with both a turned sestet and a neat closing couplet.

21 JOHN DAVIES OF HEREFORD: *'If there were, oh! an Hellespont of cream'* Another of these amazing Elizabethans, this time on his day off. Probably knocked off in ten minutes flat. Perfect English sonnet, with a sort of half-turn shoehorned in.

22 TONY HARRISON: *Guava Libra* This brilliantly risky poem juggles at least four balls in the air – feminist politics, food, sex and classical myth – with jaw-dropping skill. Despite the layout of the sestet, this is a fairly conventional Italian sonnet with four rhymes in the octave. Harrison has written many fine 'Meredithian' sonnets – sixteen lines, composed of four quatrains.

23 ROBERT SOUTHEY: *To a Goose* A nice wee parody of the Wordsworthian style, but mainly just a good cheap joke.

24 CHRISTOPHER REID: *Fly* An Italian sonnet with highly variable line lengths and odd line breaks that serve to point up the witty rhymes – also a feature of the work of Paul Muldoon, whose work the poem superficially resembles. A tiny allegory, gentle enough to be easily swallowed – most allegory is impossible to keep down.

25 LES MURRAY: *Honey Cycle* This sonnet in couplets comes from Murray's remarkable sequence 'Translations from the Natural World', in which he speaks in the voice of a number of creatures – creating a distinct idiom, a unique 'language' for each. Here the bees buzz away in a torrent of alliteration and internal rhyme, many of the lines strongly reminiscent of Anglo-Saxon verse.

26 HENRY HOWARD, EARL OF SURREY: *The Soote Season* Howard was one of the earliest English sonneteers, and is credited with having invented the 'English' form. Of which this is not a typical example! It uses only two rhymes throughout.

27 SAMUEL TAYLOR COLERIDGE: *Work without Hope* After 'Dejection: an Ode' Coleridge wrote very little poetry: this is a very late poem indeed, and in the intervening years things had clearly gone from very bad to even worse – you feel like slapping him and pointing out that he's just knocked out a fine sonnet. The awful dereliction Coleridge feels in the absence of his lyric muse seems somehow symbolised in the 'wrongness' of the inversion of the sestet and the octave.

28 TRUMBULL STICKNEY: *The Melancholy Year* Stickney died tragically young, a brain tumour killing him at thirty. The tone of

this poem is not untypical of his work: intensely sad, with a terrible note of valediction. An Italian sonnet, finely sustained in mood.

29 ELIZABETH BARRETT BROWNING: *Grief* An Italian sonnet, with the turn a line late. Barrett Browning is particularly expert at varying the rhythm of her lines by emphasising or shifting the position of the caesura (the 'break' or natural pause in the line, usually after the second or third stress) with clever punctuation. Her *Sonnets from the Portuguese* was one of the most important sonnet sequences of the nineteenth century, and is still much admired today.

30 JAMES THOMSON: *'Striving to sing glad songs, I but attain'* Best known as the author of the dark and brilliantly imaginative 'The City of Dreadful Night', James 'laughing boy' Thomson's claim to the title of Most Miserable Poet Ever is perhaps only challenged by Weldon Kees. This is grand English sonnet, married only by lines 7 and 8 where his argument goes a little astray.

31 WILLIAM MATTHEWS: *Cheap Seats, the Cincinnati Gardens, Professional Basketball, 1959* Something like a modern Miltonic, really. A fine, deceptively chatty sonnet on the singular grief of adolescent loneliness – though note how the gradient gently rises in 'for I knew none by name/among that hazy company', lifting the last lines of the poem onto a higher rhetorical plane.

32 ROBERT CRAWFORD: *Opera* An unrhymed sonnet, and a poem of open celebration: any note of irony (along with elegy, perhaps the most habitual and pervasive tone present – and therefore almost inaudible - in much contemporary poetry) is done with in the first line. The poem puns everywhere on the singing title (which just means 'work' in Italian) and by implication on the poet's typed-up sonnet itself (from the Italian 'sonetto', a little sound or song).

33 ROBERT HAYDEN: *Those Winter Sundays* An unorthodox sonnet of the 5-4-5 formation (compare Ní Chuilleanáin's 'Swineherd'). Beautifully moving final cadence; like Larkin's 'Friday Night at the Royal Station Hotel', it shows the effectiveness of upping the rhetorical ante late in the poem.

34 WALTER RALEIGH: *To His Sonne* Still better known as an adventurer, Raleigh was also a poet of the first rank. This is an exemplary English sonnet – actually quite unusual, in that it follows

the clear argumentative structure that theorists so often claim for it. Chilling, and probably written during one of his extended sabbaticals in the Tower.

35 HARTLEY COLERIDGE: *Long Time a Child* It's time to scotch one of nineteenth-century literature's most pernicious myths – that of Hartley Coleridge's mediocrity as a poet. Hartley felt entirely eclipsed by his father's reputation, but while he may not have had STC's intellectual reach, his ear was as good, if not better, and he was easily the better sonneteer – even if his subject matter was obsessively self-deprecating. Generally regarded as a great bloke and his own worst enemy.

36 WELDON KEES: *For My Daughter* One of the most unremittingly bleak poets ever to wield the pen, Kees, poet, abstract expressionist painter, jazz musician and misanthrope, simply disappeared in 1955 when his car was found abandoned near the Golden Gate bridge in San Francisco. This poem demonstrates his early fondness for vanishing acts: the daughter in the poem evaporates before our eyes in the last line. The sonnet has a very unconventional rhyme scheme and no turn, as it consists of one *big* turn; the language is rather anachronistic, and almost Baudelairian in its spleen.

37 MICHAEL DONAGHY: *The Brother* An unrhymed sonnet, with the turn a line later than normal. Note especially the clever riddle of 'the only man at my wedding not wearing a tie', and the astonishing concision of the last line – forcing the reader to do a disturbing double-take, just like the optical illusion the poet has just described.

38 R. S. THOMAS: *The Bright Field* In this unrhymed free verse Italian sonnet Thomas – a Welsh Anglican priest – demonstrates there's an art in telling as well as showing. The bright field seems to become no more or less than the sonnet itself, a moment of elucidation.

39 JOHN CLARE: *Noon* An early Clare poem written when he was about twenty-six – an English sonnet with, as was usual for him, no punctuation, never mind a turn. As with many of his poems, you have the impression of it being written in real time, with Clare starting with the first line and ending shortly after with the last. There is never anything resembling an argument in Clare, as he was to some extent a *naif* – but this gives the best of his poetry an unaffected vivacity and charm. His habit of excluding himself from the picture lends some of

his nature poems a mystical radiance, uninterrupted by any other presence but that of his subject.

40 WILLIAM SOUTAR: *The Halted Moment* If evidence was needed that Soutar, routinely omitted from all the big anthologies, was a poet of the first order, then this little triumph of a sonnet should supply it. The use of the third person is cleverly enlisted to make the reader complicit in the scene; to have written the poem in the first person would have turned it into the 'sensitive soul' routine. A five-rhyme Italian sonnet.

41 DANTE GABRIEL ROSSETTI: *'A Sonnet is a moment's monument'* When sonneteers have nothing to write about, they write sonnets about sonnets, and it would be easy to fill another book with their efforts: Keats, Robinson, Wordsworth (2) and even Burns have all written them. This is one of the best: an Italian sonnet with a closing couplet, Rossetti's notion of the sonnet as a coin, paid to assuage a 'Power', whether love or death, is quite brilliant.

42 THOMAS BASTARD: *Ad Lectorem de Subiecto Operis Sui* Bastard published his only book, *Chrestoleros*, in 1598, to considerable ridicule – from which he seems not to have recovered, dying, half-mad, twenty years later in a debtor's prison. To judge from this elegant English sonnet, his critics were a bit hasty.

43 EDWIN MORGAN: *Opening the Cage* In spinning Cage's dictum out to sonnet length, Morgan constructs the zen equivalent of the shaggy dog story. Unusual rhyme scheme, involving 'it' a lot. Only joking.

44 PATRICK KAVANAGH: *Inniskeen Road: July Evening* This is about as good as it gets – effortless rhymes, effortless accommodation of natural speech to the form – and that lovely pun on 'blooming'. Fine witty poem on the predicament of the provincial aesthete.

45 GEOFFREY HILL: *The Laurel Axe* Just about everyone agrees that Hill is a major poet, but just about everyone except George Steiner wishes he was a bit less hard work: his poems are often like rooms so crammed with exquisite and unusual furniture it's impossible to actually walk around in them. Still, he makes the most magnificent noise you're likely to hear: this is a superb Italian sonnet, as usual, packed to the rafters with dazzling images. As a vision of England, though, platonic or otherwise . . . hmm.

46 TOM PAULIN: *In the Lost Province* Paulin is widely regarded as the most politically sophisticated of our contemporary poets, a reputation evidenced in the subtlety of this unrhymed Italian sonnet. Brookeborough was a staunch Ulster Unionist politician. 'Leviathan' refers both to the biblical sea-monster and to the state in Hobbes' famous treatise, in which he argued that men should accept an absolute power above them that would prevent them from acting in their own narrow self-interest, so protecting them from themselves and from each other.

47 CHARLOTTE SMITH: *Written in the Church Yard at Middleton in Sussex* Smith takes a lot of the credit for bringing round the sonnet when it had all but breathed its last, and was considerably influential in its subsequent adoption by the Romantics. This poem hangs a lot of energetic description on a clear argument so neatly, we're almost unaware it being made.

48 EDWARD THOMAS: *February Afternoon* A well-wrought Italian sonnet, written when Thomas was on convalescent leave. We can infer the state of Thomas's mind from a letter to his wife written around the same time: 'Well, I can't write any more. I am only fit to lie and listen to Mother reading Revelations.' Bless . . .

49 PERCY BYSSHE SHELLEY: *Ozymandias* The brilliance of Shelley's sonnet on the vanity of the tyrant's power lies in his simply *presenting* an irony, rather than adopting any irony of tone. Ozymandias was the praenomen of Ramses II (better known as Ramses the Great), third king of the nineteenth dynasty of Egypt, where many colossal statues of him are still to be found.

50 MARILYN HACKER: *Mythology* A witty feminist rewriting of the Ulysses myth – an Italian sonnet, with a slightly late turn in line 9. The variation of the placement of stress within the pentameter line is virtuosic: there's barely one line that states the i.p. explicitly, yet its rhythm is as strongly felt as that of a jazz drummer under a soloist; the i.p. of late Shakespeare makes an instructive comparison. Hacker has also written some notable sonnet sequences.

51 W. B. YEATS: *Leda and the Swan* A great poem, apparently on the collision of divine and mortal worlds; but given that Leda was the mother of Helen of Troy – to whom Yeats habitually compared his beloved Maud Gonne – it can also be read as another anguished love

poem, written at a knight's move. An Italian sonnet, with a heartstopping break halfway through line 11.

52 THOMAS HARDY: *She, to Him (iii)* An early English sonnet of Hardy's – and rather Elizabethan in tone. There's only one visual conceit, the weather vane 'true to the wind that kissed ere canker came', but Hardy sets it in the argument of the poem like a gem in a ring.

53 MICHAEL DRAYTON: *'Since there's no help, come let us kiss and part'* Drayton wrote one of the major Elizabethan sonnet cycles, *Ideas Mirrour*. Another Anglo-Italian, really: look at the brave face of the octave, then at how the poet's resolve wavers and collapses entirely in the sestet; a very *human* poem.

54 GEORGE GASCOIGNE: *'You must not wonder though you think it strange'* Yet another great early renaissance man – the usual mix of politician / soldier of fortune / man of letters. Gascoigne is notable for having foreshadowed the English sonnet sequence in *A Hunderth Sundrie Flowers*, his first published work, seventeen years before Sidney's *Astrophel and Stella*. This is a fine poem, but it finishes on line 12 – a good example of superfluous couplet syndrome, a.k.a. the 'English disease', in action.

55 DYLAN THOMAS: *'Their faces shone under some radiance'* An early Thomas poem, this – a loose sonnet with a scatter of half-rhymes, and a late turn on line 10. The last line is quite mysterious, and extends the withdrawn blessing of the light to the wider world, where it seems to have held death temporarily at bay.

56 THOMAS HOOD: *Death* An English sonnet from the author of the famous proto-protest-poem 'The Song of the Shirt', and perhaps the only man ever to have been sent to Dundee to improve his health. A finely argued poem that, cleverly, seems to have shot its bolt at the end of the second quatrain; but after the turn, the poet introduces the idea of an even more thorough effacement.

57 CHRISTINA ROSSETTI: *After Death* Rossetti would have followed Alfred, Lord Tennyson as Poet Laureate had she not developed a fatal cancer in 1891; no woman had held the laureateship before – and her succession to the post would have set an important precedent. This beautifully executed Italian sonnet is almost Dickinsonesque in its weirdness; it has the air of an oddly masochistic adolescent fantasy.

58 JAMIE MCKENDRICK: *Ye Who Enter In* An unrhymed sonnet, (very) loosely after the Spanish of Antonio Machado; it ticks along with a neat satire on Dante, and his rather convenient poet's version of hell – until the last line, funny and chilling with the hint of the real thing.

59 EDWIN ARLINGTON ROBINSON: *Karma* Robinson, perhaps the greatest American sonneteer, set many of his poems in the imaginary 'Tilbury Town' in New England: they are often the sort of brilliantly perceptive psychological portrait we see in 'Karma'. He almost always rhymes his Italian sonnets ABBAABBA in the octave, then uses three rhymes, variously distributed, for the sestet.

60 CIARAN CARSON: *Finding the Ox* This is more of a French sonnet than an Italian. It's written in alexandrines – very unusual in English, but as central to French verse as i.p. is to poetry in English: in French prosody, it's a line of twelve syllables, though because English prosody is stress- and not syllable-based it comes out very different in this language. The poem is from Carson's *The Twelfth of Never*, a real *tour-de-force* sequence of seventy-seven alexandrine sonnets, strongly influenced by the French Symbolists, whom he has also translated.

61 EILÉAN NÍ CHUILLEANÁIN: *Swineherd* The 4-6-4 formation. The poem gets more surreal as it unravels, but so quietly you hardly notice. Look again at the last stanza: isn't it *strange?*

62 JOHN BERRYMAN: *'I dreamt he drove me back to the asylum'* The terrible pathos of this poem convinces you that this *was* a real dream, not Berryman making one up. An Italian sonnet, effortlessly accommodating a very conversational syntax.

63 GLYN MAXWELL: *My Turn* An odd sort of sonnet in couplets, if you can call it a sonnet at all. Dark, oppressive, paranoid, vaguely surreal and wonderfully atmospheric, this was the first poem in Maxwell's first book, and it can be read as an announcement of his own arrival: starting up the abandoned roundabout, then staying on it.

64 WILFRED BLUNT: *Farewell to Juliet* A painfully bourgeois effort in a lot of ways, but he couldn't help it. In Blunt's defence he was a vociferous opponent of colonial exploitation in India, a vocal anti-imperialist and supporter of oppressed small nations. A nice English sonnet – and very affecting, if a little bit soppy.

65 JOHN KEATS: *'When I have fears that I may cease to be'* In any other poet one might read the first four lines as conceited and self-important in the extreme, but in Keats' case it all seems perfectly reasonable. An English sonnet, with a small turn on line 9 as his beloved enters the picture, and a much more emphatic turn halfway through line 12.

66 EMILY DICKINSON: *'I read my sentence – steadily'* Despite the occasional absurd claims made on her behalf as a great metricist, Dickinson was almost incapable of conceiving of poetry in anything other than ballad meter; a formal *naif* she may have been, but she combined this with the intellectual power of a John Donne. This sonnet was probably produced entirely by accident – lines 9 and 10 are each two lines of a ballad stanza conflated into one – though it turns beautifully between lines 8 and 9. The poem received an extraordinary setting by the late Norwegian singer Radka Toneff.

67 JOSEPH BLANCO WHITE: *To Night* 'To Night' manages to sound superficially like a bad Romantic sonnet – you sometimes get the impression that these poets would have simply exploded it if hadn't been for the exclam – though it's actually a very good poem. An Italian sonnet with a couplet at the end, it's a textbook example of how that particular variant should be handled: the turn is good, but the conceit in the couplet is quite terrific – and all the more effective for having been delayed so long. A favourite poem of Coleridge's, incidentally.

68 SAMUEL DANIEL: *'Care-charmer Sleep, son of the sable Night'* This is sonnet xlv from Daniel's sonnet sequence Delia. An English sonnet in which the turn is ignored in order to extend its supremely well-sustained moan down the length of the poem, although it's cursorily flagged with the initial stressed syllable of 'Cease' in line 9. The imperative mood is an old trick of the trade, and allows poets to ignore the first weak syllable of the pentameter whenever they feel like it.

69 ALFRED, LORD TENNYSON: *Now Sleeps the Crimson Petal* This poem is embedded in Tennyson's *The Princess*, reasonably described by one commentator as an 'anti-feminist fantasia'. This wonderful sonnet rises above it and sings out beyond it, though: with its anaphora and epistrophe (the repetition of the initial part of the line, and the repetition of the last) it's more of an unrhymed lyric than a true sonnet, perhaps, but who's counting.

70 PAUL MULDOON: *The Princess and the Pea* Muldoon is one of the contemporary masters of the sonnet. The symbol of unity that the

sonnet supplies chimes well with Muldoon's great project, which is to prove that everything is everything else by demonstrating the interchangeability of all terms, no matter how disparate: Muldoon will sometimes yoke the most outlandish words together in rhyme, or separate the rhymes by many lines, many pages or even whole *books*: thus rhyme becomes a structural as well as a local device. This is a more conventional take on the form – a brilliant Italian sonnet with Muldoon's customary variable line-length, and things taking, literally, a very nasty turn.

71 EDNA ST VINCENT MILLAY: *'I, being born a woman and distressed'* Another great sonneteer, here with an acidly witty poem in the form of an extended kiss-off line that many woman might find handy to memorise and keep about their person. The high ironic tone is so well achieved in the first few lines, you can imagine the poor sod she's addressing momentarily thinking she might be serious. A technically immaculate Italian sonnet, with a turn to die for.

72 ANTHONY HECHT: *An Old Malediction* But nicely updated; an unrhymed sonnet, and no point in having a turn here, since curses have to be relentless. Hecht is very classical in his language, and while lines like 'the saline latitudes of incontinent grief' might sound like a parody of Horation high irony, such phrases are very much an everyday part of his elegant armoury.

73 ROBERT GARIOCH: *Elegy* An Italian sonnet, divided into two quatrains and two tercets, with a great punchline. Garioch was a prolific sonneteer, and translated many of the Roman dialect poet Guiseppe Belli's sonnets into Scots.

74 GEORGE MACKAY BROWN: *The Death of Peter Esson* The Orcadian poet had the gift of allowing everything he describes to stand in its own free space, its own silence – and this is a typically unfussy and clear-sighted use of the English sonnet form. The quatrains refer to each of the dead man's three occupations in turn, and only in the last couplet does the voice of the poet quietly intrude.

75 RICHARD FANSHAWE: *The Fall* Fanshawe is principally famous for his translation of Camões great epic *Os Lusiadas*; this English sonnet is a version from the Spanish of Gongora. Fanshawe may have also had in mind the fall from grace of Thomas Wentworth, Earl of Strafford, who was executed in 1641, a scapegoat for Charles I's failure to put down the Scottish rebellion.

76 CATHERINE DYER: *Epitaph on the Monument of Sir William Dyer at Colmworth* The only poem we have by Lady Catherine Dyer, and surely one of the most beautiful and moving epitaphs ever written. The fact that the metre is uneven and there's a line missing (presumably no rhyme could be found for *cold*) seems to make no difference; whether this was intended as a sonnet or not, it's as true to the spirit of the form as anything else in this book – look, for example at the gentle, gracious turn on line 9.

77 JOHN MILTON: *On His Deceased Wife* Milton's second wife, Catherine, died in childbirth only a year after their marriage. Alcestis, daughter of Pelias, gave up her life in exchange for that of her husband Admetus. Heracles later rescued her from Hades. This is a typical 'Miltonic' sonnet, with no turn between octave and sestet.

78 GWENDOLYN BROOKS: *The Rites for Cousin Vit* Vit exuberantly destroys the solemnity of her own funeral, and bullies the poem into something openly celebratory. An Italian sonnet, though it purposely doesn't utilise the turn, which would only have been an interruption.

79 SIMON ARMITAGE: *Poem* The determinedly flat tone of this English sonnet is signalled in the absolute matter-of-factness of the title: the reader is then presented with an accumulating pile of contradictory evidence. This refusal to simplify or caricature in order to arrive at an easy moral judgement is typical of Armitage's work, and to some extent this is a manifesto piece. The sonnet is unusual in that its rhymes are all assonantal (i.e., rhymed on vowels rather than consonants.)

80 W. H. AUDEN: *Who's Who* One of Auden's favourite themes – how the hero turns out to be a regular guy, really. Or at least hanker after one. Great use of the semicolon in the sestet in echoing the syntax of the octave, and so prompting the reader to contrast the two CVs.

81 MICHAEL LONGLEY: *Grace Darling* An English sonnet, and an object lesson in how to handle the couplet. Longley's poem is a good example of how, in elegy, the use of the second person rather than the third lends a real intimacy to the speech – and a sad frisson, because we know the person isn't there to be addressed.

82 EDMUND SPENSER: *'One day I wrote her name upon the strand'* Spenser innovated this way of interweaving the rhymes of the English quatrains as a good compromise between the four rhymes of

the strict Italian and the seven of the English. The rhyme scheme is ABABBCBCCDCDEE. The idea of the verse as a stay against time – specifically, as a way of immortalising the love of the poet – was a very popular theme in Elizabethan sonnets.

83 WENDY COPE: from *Strugnell's Sonnets* This is the self-styled 'Bard of Tulse Hill' Jason Strugnell's improvement of Shakespeare's sonnet 55: 'Not marble, nor the gilded monuments / Of princes, shall outlive this powerful rhyme . . .'

84 WILLIAM SHAKESPEARE: *'That time of year thou mayst in me behold'* Leaving yourself able to choose only one of Shakespeare's sonnets is clearly the most serious flaw in the plan of this book; it's important to convey, since I can't present more evidence than this single poem, that he really *was* the greatest sonneteer who ever lived. One of the most obvious tokens of greatness in a poet is in the infinite variety and subtlety of their syntax, which betrays the sophistication of thought behind the poem (impeccable music we can take for granted: there have been many more poets with pitch-perfect hearing); this is something, I'd contend, that we find in all poets of genius – Donne, Dickinson, Yeats, Auden, Bishop and Heaney. It's also why a poem of Shakespeare's can, initially, be quite difficult to understand; many people attribute this to the unfamiliarity of Elizabethan English, but the poetry of his contemporaries is generally simpler to follow. Anyway, to the sonnet: it argues that the poet's decrepitude should mean that the young man to whom it is addressed should love him all the more, time being so short. An exercise in wishful thinking if ever there was one – but what a poem!

85 EZRA POUND: *A Virginal* This Italian sonnet is a self-conscious attempt to imitate the cadences of seventeenth-century poetry, Donne in particular – though there are echoes of the earlier Wyatt, and the troubadour poetry in which Pound was immersed at the time. And rather good it is, too: the language might be deliberately anachronistic, but the feeling immediately recognisable – that after the beloved has left, you *must* be left alone to savour the lingering taste of her . . .

86 THOMAS WYATT: *'Whoso list to hunt, I know where is an hind'* Wyatt, along with Howard of Surrey, was largely responsible for popularising the sonnet in England; this, like many of his sonnets, is a free imitation of the Petrarch, his primary inspiration in the sonnet form. The 'hind' Wyatt refers to is, we all like to believe, Anne Boleyn –

Wyatt's lover who Henry VIII (presumably 'Caesar' in the poem) claimed for himself. Wyatt set the trend for using the sonnet as a means of elaborating a single conceit – that of the hunt, in this case – throughout the poem.

87 ROBERT LOWELL: *'To Speak of the Woe that is in Marriage'* This dramatic monologue manages to work amazingly well considering the despairing wife sounds just like Robert Lowell: a window on two horribly warped lives. Another sonnet in couplets – the rhymes are quite brilliant – with the turn, such as it is, after line 9 rather than 8.

88 DOUGLAS DUNN: *Modern Love* The title echoes that of Meredith's famous sonnet-sequence – but whereas his was a tale of marital torment, this is clearly bliss; a lovely weightless sonnet with a last line that in any other poem might have sounded bathetic, but here sounds like a kind of refused cadence, keeping the poem suspended in time and space.

89 GEORGE MEREDITH: *Lucifer in Starlight* Meredith is best known for his semi-autobiographical sequence *Modern Love*, in which he employed a sixteen-line sonnet of four quatrains, thereafter known as the 'Meredithian' sonnet. This wonderfully cinematic and scary poem is an immaculate five-rhyme Italian sonnet.

90 FULKE GREVILLE: *'Satan, no woman, yet a wandering spirit'* Not very PC, granted, but this is a brilliantly-argued sonnet that unfolds with a complete inevitability. Greville was fond of using the three quatrains of the English sonnet as stanzas proper, arranging the poem in strict episodes.

91 MARK ALEXANDER BOYD: *Sonet* This Italian sonnet is the only poem Boyd ever wrote in Scots – he worked exclusively in Latin. Mind you, if you're only going to write one, it might as well be one of the finest lyrics of the age. The 'twa gods', of course, are blind Cupid and Venus.

92 PHILIP SYDNEY: *'With how sad steps, O Moon, thou climb'st the skies'* Sidney started the trend for sonnet sequences in England with the publication of *Astrophel and Stella* in 1590. The clever device of the interrogation of the moon allows the poet to express his bitterness at one remove – in questions rather than peevish statements. Like Wyatt, Sidney wrote sonnets that were half Italian and half English – always closing the sestet with a couplet.

93 PHILIP LARKIN: *Friday Night in the Royal Station Hotel* An Italian sonnet with the break a line late. Note especially the dramatic shift of tone in the last two lines, as the poet suddenly classicises his predicament.

94 LOUIS MACNEICE: *Sunday Morning* MacNeice's rhythm is a perfectly inimitable miracle, somewhere between triple-meter and speech-rhythm, and always turns to doggerel in the hands of anyone else who attempts it. Whether it's deliberate or not, it's interesting to note how the division of the two stanzas echoes precisely the ratio of the working week to the weekend; it also emphasises the poem's disturbing lop-sidedness. A sonnet in couplets.

95 CAROL ANN DUFFY: *Prayer* The shipping forecast has long been a nice off-the-peg number for poets, but no one can have used it so poignantly as Duffy in this masterfully quiet English sonnet. Note the 'some days' / 'some nights' opposition of the first two quatrains, and the gentle breaking of the iambic rhythm at the start of the third.

96 GEORGE HERBERT: *Prayer* One of the great masters of the sonnet, with one of the great sonnets. The poem is an inspired litany, and rises in the last three lines to a near-hallucinogenic intensity; then this zodiac of marvels seems suddenly sucked back into the little box of the poem in the last two words, just in time before it clicks shut. An English sonnet, and being a list-poem, no place for the turn. Compare Barnabe Barnes' 'A blast of wind, a momentary breath'.

97 BARNABE BARNES: *'A blast of wind, a momentary breath'* A list-poem bearing more than a passing resemblance to Herbert's 'Prayer', which it seems to have influenced; it differs in that whereas the key to Herbert's poem is in the title, Barnes' poem is laid out like a riddle, the answer withheld until the couplet.

98 RICHARD WILBUR: *Praise in Summer* This is a fine poem against the poet's bad habit of wilfully estranging the world in order to put in place sufficient distance to praise it: this is probably a fault of every poet at some time or another in their careers. An English sonnet, with the turn delayed by a line. Wilbur is occasionally co-opted into the (singularly) American 'New Formalist' movement, but he is resolutely 'Old Formalist' – a poet whose roots go deep back into the tradition.

99 ELIZABETH BISHOP: *Sonnet* Typical Bishop, not a word wasted. She would often pin up poems in front of her desk, a line or so short of

completion; some might stay there for ten years before they were finished. You'd think she could have just made it up. Ho ho. An unusual sonnet – free-rhymed, using a two-stress accentual line, the position of the turn reversed, so it occurs between lines 6 and 7.

100 GERARD MANLEY HOPKINS: *'As kingfishers catch fire'* Hopkins' is a unique music: every detail is so heavily drenched in alliteration and internal rhyme (look here, for example, at how that *-ing* sound bells throughout the octave like an angelus, and how each line of the sestet seems to have a different consonantal signature) that occasionally the poem can drown in its own lovely racket. Here, though, the argument is beautifully clear. A very strict Italian sonnet in its rhymes and turn, though as usual, Hopkins' take on the pentameter is all his own.

101 WILLIAM BLAKE: *To the Evening Star* This lovely hymn is Blake's only sonnet, as far as I can make out. Whether he was conscious of writing it as a sonnet is hard to say – there are no rhymes, there's no turn, and the metre is all over the place. The appearance of the Lion signals that we are in Blakeland, just in case you were thinking it was England.

102 NORMAN MACCAIG: *Rag and Bone* It's been said that MacCaig was a major poet who wrote only minor poems, but reading his *Collected Poems* is like tipping out a bucket of gemstones on the carpet. When asked how long it took him to write a poem, MacCaig would invariably reply 'two fags'. Whether this great little extemporisation took him *that* long is open to debate, as is the question of its sonnet status. But again, who cares.

103 SEAMUS HEANEY: *The Skylight* No one does the heft and feel of things like Heaney; his poetic scales are so finely calibrated you could weigh air and light in them. This is a wonderful Italian sonnet about no more than the thing it describes – things being where most of the deepest mysteries are, and where most of the best poets find them.

ACKNOWLEDGEMENTS

The editor and publishers gratefully acknowledge permission to re-print copyright material in this book as follows:

SIMON ARMITAGE: Faber and Faber Ltd for 'Poem' from *Kid;* W. H. AUDEN: Faber and Faber Ltd for 'Who's Who' from *Collected Poems;* JOHN BERRYMAN: Faber and Faber Ltd for 'No. 79' from *The Dream Songs;* ELIZABETH BISHOP: 'Sonnet' from *The Complete Poems 1927–1979* by Elizabeth Bishop, copyright © 1979, 1983 by Alice Helen Methfessel, reprinted by permission of Farrar, Straus & Giroux, Inc.; GEORGE MACKAY BROWN: John Murray for 'The Death of Peter Esson' from *Selected Poems;* WENDY COPE: Faber and Faber Ltd for 'Strugnell's Sonnet (iv)' from *Making Cocoa for Kingsley Amis* (1986); MICHAEL DONAGHY: 'The Brother' from *Errata* (OUP, 1993) by kind permission of the author; CAROL ANN DUFFY: Anvil Press Poetry Ltd for 'Prayer' from *Mean Time* (1993); DOUGLAS DUNN: Faber and Faber Ltd for 'Modern Love' from *Selected Poems;* ROBERT FROST: for 'The Silken Tent', the Estate of Robert Frost, the editor of *Collected Poems of Robert Frost,* Edward Connery Latham, and Jonathan Cape; ROBERT GRAVES: Carcanet Press Ltd for 'In Her Praise' from *Collected Poems* (1986); TONY HARRISON: Gordon Dickerson on behalf of the author for 'Guava Librea' from *Selected Poems* (Penguin, 1984); SEAMUS HEANEY: Faber and Faber Ltd for 'The Skylight' from *Opened Ground: Poems 1966–1996* (1998); WELDON KEES: Faber and Faber Ltd for 'For My Daughter' from *Selected Poems* (1993); PHILIP LARKIN: Faber and Faber Ltd for 'Friday Night in the Royal Station Hotel' from *Collected Poems* (1988); ROBERT LOWELL: Faber and Faber Ltd for 'To Speak of the Woe that is in Marriage' from *Selected Poems;* NORMAN MACCAIG: Random House UK Ltd on behalf of the Estate of Norman MacCaig for 'Rag and Bone' from *Collected Poems* (Chatto and Windus, 1985); LOUIS MACNEICE: David Higham Associates for 'Sunday Morning' from *Collected Poems* (Faber, 1966); GLYN MAXWELL: Bloodaxe Books for 'My Turn' from *Rest for the Wicked* (1995); JAMIE MCKENDRICK: 'Ye Who Enter In' from *Kiosk on the Brink* (OUP, 1993) by kind permission of the author; PAUL MULDOON: Faber and Faber Ltd for 'The Princess and the Pea' from *Why Brownlee Left;* EILEAN NI CHUILLEANAIN: 'Swineherd' from *The Second Voyage* (1986), by kind permission of the author and The Gallery

[121]

Press; TOM PAULIN: Faber and Faber Ltd for 'In the Lost Province' from *The Strange Museum*; EZRA POUND: Faber and Faber Ltd for 'A Virginal' from *Selected Poems*; CRAIG RAINE: to David Godwin Associates for 'Arsehole' from *Rich* (1984); CHRISTOPHER REID: Faber and Faber Ltd for 'Fly' from *Expanded Universes* (1996); JO SHAPCOTT: for 'Muse' from *Phrase Book* (OUP, 1992), by kind permission of the author; WALLACE STEVENS: Faber and Faber Ltd for 'The Poem that Took the Place of a Mountain' from *Selected Poems* (1953); DYLAN THOMAS: David Higham Associates for 'Their faces shone under some radiance' from *Collected Poems*; R. S. THOMAS: Macmillan Publishers Ltd for 'The Bright Field' from *Later Poems*, R. S. Thomas (Macmillan, 1983); RICHARD WILBUR: Faber and Faber Ltd for 'Praise in Summer' from *Collected Poems*; W. B. YEATS: for 'Leda and the Swan' from *The Collected Poems of W. B. Yeats* (Macmillan, 1985), by permission of A. P. Watt Ltd on behalf of Michael B. Yeats.

The publishers have made every effort to secure permission to reprint material protected by copyright. They will be pleased to make good any omissions brought to their attention in future printings of this book.

INDEX OF POETS

INDEX OF FIRST LINES

They are lang deid, folk that I used to ken 73
This is no dream 70
This they know well: the Goddess yet abides 4
Thou fair-hair'd angel of the evening 101
Three thinges there bee that prosper up apace 34
Through the open french window the warm sun 20
Throw all your stagey chandeliers in wheelbarrows and move them north 32
To plumb the depths of hell and meet 58
Two voices are there: one is of the deep 14
Wha hasna turn'd inby a sunny street 40
What well-heeled knuckle-head, straight from the unisex 72
'When all this is over,' said the swineherd 61
When I have fears that I may cease to be 65
When I kiss you in all the folding places 5
Whoso list to hunt, I know where is an hind 86
With how sad steps, O Moon, thou climb'st the skies 92
You must not wonder though you think it strange 54
You were the one for skylights. I opposed 103